TURNING HEARTS

TURNING HEARTS

THE PROMISE AND PRACTICE OF SPIRITUAL PARENTING

RICKIE D. MOORE

Moore, Rickie D.
Turning hearts : the promise and practice of spiritual parenting / Rickie D. Moore. – Franklin, Tennessee : Seedbed Publishing, ©2025.

pages ; cm.

ISBN: 9798888001844 (paperback)
ISBN: 9798888001851 (epub)
ISBN: 9798888001868 (pdf)
OCLC: 1529967430

1. Discipling (Christianity) 2. Witness bearing (Christianity) 3. Spiritual formation.
4. Christian education of children. 5. Mentoring--Religious aspects--Christianity.
6. Parenting--Religious aspects--Christianity. I. Title.

BV4520.M667 2025   253   2025943045

SEEDBED PUBLISHING
Franklin, Tennessee
Seedbed.com

For my Jean

CONTENTS

Preface   ix

INTRODUCTION: A Personal Story   1

CHAPTER 1: The Biblical Roots of Spiritual
   Parenting   21

CHAPTER 2: Telling Stories to Our Children   49

CHAPTER 3: Listening to Our Children When
   They Are Coming of Age   63

CHAPTER 4: Telling Our Stories to Our
   Questioning Children   83

CHAPTER 5: Our Weak Points Turned into
   Strong Links   107

CHAPTER 6: The Spirit of Spiritual Parenting   133

Select Bibliography with Annotations   161

PREFACE

My greatest resource for writing a book on spiritual parenting comes by way of the actual spiritual parents I have had in my life—faithful mothers and fathers who turned their hearts toward me and drew my heart to turn toward them. Even long before I came to realize it, my close relationships with these beloved elders were always a vital dimension of my relationship to God.

In time, I came to realize how such heart-to-heart turnings were God's chosen way of linking generations together in His covenant and forming what could be described as God's intentionally designed channel through which life-giving gifts of the old to the young and the young to the old were, from the beginning, meant to be shared. This realization led me to a very deep conviction: the hearts of the young, whether they know it or not, long for the gift of blessing, and the hearts of the old, whether they know it or not, yearn for the gift of honor. The curse of our time is how badly and pervasively this God-ordained heart channel has been blocked and broken and, thus, how dreadfully the flow of honor to elders and blessing to children has been depleted and even deleted from our consciousness.

This is all the more reason that I owe an immeasurable debt of honor to the spiritual parents, who, against all odds during these times, have found their way into my life and taken me into their hearts. I would hope that this book could in some small way reflect the enormous honor I have in my heart for them and the inexpressible gratitude I feel for all the blessings they have bestowed upon me.

As I look back on my seventy-one years, I am overtaken by the thought that I have had far more than my share of spiritual parents. Psalm 127 declares that children are "like arrows in the hand of a warrior," bringing blessing upon the one whose "quiver [is] full of them" (vv. 3–5). How blessed I have been to be taken up and placed in the quivers of so many! The list begins, as God intended, of course, with Ernest and Doris Moore, who were spiritual as well as natural parents to me. The list extends to several godly loved ones in my extended family. Following them is a steady line of other spiritual elders who have come into my life by way of the church, the family of God. First, there was the small Michigan congregation in which I grew up as a child, where I was adopted by true fathers and mothers of the faith, such as Brother and Sister Dodd (as we called them), Brother and Sister Sizemore, Brother and Sister Davidson, Brother and Sister Chandler, Sister Parks, Sister Sue Vloch, Dave and Joyce Kirk, Calvin Orbin, and Bedford Smith. Then there were teachers and mentors in my coming-of-age years in Tennessee, such as Jim and Margaret Hamilton, John Sims, Eddie and Irma Williams, Lynn Stone, Roland Sharp, Steve Land, and Marcia Anderson—all of whom engraved indelible and eternal imprints upon my life.

There are four other individuals who stand out for special mention, for they claim a special place not only in the preface of this book but also in the preface of my life's calling—a place grounded in their own life's calling to be spiritual parents.

Margaret Gaines became a spiritual mother to me during my own life passage into parenthood. She opened her soul to me, and through this opening poured a stream of inspired wisdom that has lasted a lifetime. I tell the heart of this story in chapter 3.

Robert Crick became a spiritual father to me during my life passage into my vocation as a teacher. Bob had served as a military chaplain during the Vietnam War and had become a highly skilled clinical pastoral education supervisor. He was the dean of ministry at the seminary where I was hired to begin my teaching career. Fresh out of grad school, I was an "expert" (so they said) at reading biblical texts. Bob was an expert at reading people. He read me. I was on a head trip, but Bob invited me to join him on a heart journey. He opened his heart to me and found his way into mine, beyond all my self-protection, posturing, and pretense. Bob showed me the probing and, at times, pain-inducing compassion of an earthly father that opened me to a much deeper knowing of the heavenly Father. He told me one time that most people come to their sense of personhood early in adulthood and then spend the rest of their lives protecting it, whereas a much smaller number spend their entire lifetime growing and developing as a person. Now in his nineties, Bob has continued to grow as a path-charting spiritual elder in my life. I still want to be like him when I grow up.

David Dehner became a spiritual father to me during my life passage into ministry in the church. As a young leader in a small-group ministry, I hit my first sizable ministerial snag when two leaders over me in the Lord got into a conflict with each other. I was like a child with parents who were well on their way to breaking up. I found myself saying to a close friend and peer in the same ministry group, "I wish I had a leader who could bring our two leaders together." My friend then suggested I consider seeking the advice of a certain man in our congregation, a retired pastor he knew named David Dehner.

I finally reached out to this older man, introduced myself, and asked him out to a lunch meeting, where I cautiously described my dilemma without naming any names. After listening intently to my story, he finally leaned forward and spoke to me these words: "Blessed are the peacemakers" (Matt. 5:9a). Those words immediately pierced my heart to the point of drawing tears, although I did not know how or why I started crying. He went on to say that he suspected that the situation that had led me to reach out to him was more of a providential prompt for getting us to spend some time together rather than the main point of our lunch meeting. And he was right. We began to spend time together, week after week and year after year. All told, our relationship lasted about a decade. After a heart attack took his life in 1995, I was preparing the eulogy for his funeral and remembered his words to me on that first day I met with him. And the truth he had spoken came into searing focus. I had wanted to find an elder to help me with a problem, only to find out over time that my problem was that I needed an elder.

The spiritual inheritance that David Dehner bequeathed to me is far too much to tell. But there was one treasured moment in David's time as my spiritual elder that is too significant and revelatory to be left unmentioned. One night we were on a road trip to visit a young man who had been transferred from our county jail in Tennessee to a federal prison in Alabama. During a time of deep sharing, David suddenly looked at me and said, "When I see you, I see the end of me." How affirming to hear his thought that I could one day wear his mantle! But then, quite to my surprise, he said, "And if I let it, that would really bother me." Then he smiled the most beautiful smile and said, "But I've decided not to let it bother me." I treasure that moment because I have come to realize that David was giving up a deep secret that those of the older generation are ever tempted to keep from those of the younger generation: their fear of the younger taking their place. And this well-kept secret is precisely what keeps the older generation from blessing the next generation. If this book succeeds in disclosing anything worth learning about spiritual parenting, it will be due in no small part to the spirit of David Dehner, whose father's heart was openly and honestly turned to me to the very end.

Frances Brannen became a spiritual mother to me during my life passage into what I would now call my golden years of being a grandfather—both in my family and in the household of faith. Frances is the sister of my wife's late mother. For many years, Frances and her husband served as missionaries, first in South America and later in Africa, helping to establish a Bible college in Kenya. During most of my married life, I knew her as "Aunt Frances"—a favorite aunt of my wife, Jean. But then came the years of her so-called retirement, and I watched her ministry climb to new levels of impact and gravity. No longer able to go and serve people far away, she increasingly has become a center of gravity, drawing people from all directions to come to her and sit in her presence.

Her retirement home is located on the route that takes me to the Lee University campus where I continue to serve now on a voluntary basis in my own retirement years as senior advisor to "Lee Prayer," the university's student prayer ministry. This assignment has led to many other spin-off assignments on campus and beyond. Frances has shown me that when you cease to be fully employed, you can still be fully *de*ployed in the work of God's kingdom. More times than I can count, I have been on my way to the campus, carrying the burdens of the day's assignments, and then suddenly realized that a brief stop by Frances's house is just what I need. She would meet me at the back door with a welcoming smile, and stepping into her kitchen would be like stepping into a sanctuary—because that is exactly what it is. She would invite me to sit down at a little table just inside the back door. And it would take only a few short minutes for

Frances to take in the burden I'm carrying and then take it to the Lord in prayer—a prayer full of the discernment, authority, and glory of someone who walks close to Jesus. Every time I sit with her, she turns that table into an altar, and I leave with a heart that is full and running over with the blessing that only a spiritual mother can give.

Frances is a spiritual mother to both me and my wife, Jean, and she has helped us realize that God has made the two of us to be one in our call to be spiritual parents. It should have been a no-brainer all along that our fruitfulness together is many times more than any fruitfulness we ever could have had apart from one another. A mother changes everything.

So, it is altogether right that the name of my wife, Jean, appears alone on the dedication page of this book. Her life infuses all the other pages. And together we bless all those who read these pages, especially those who are themselves hearing and answering the call to be spiritual parents.

I finally want to express my gratitude to all the folks on the Seedbed team, whose publishing mission has given this book the very best and most fitting place to come forth. Their wonderful work has made this book much better. The shortcomings that remain are my own. Special thanks go to J. D. Walt, Andy Miller, Andrew Dragos, Mike Cowart, and David Thomas, who initially encouraged me to consider pursuing this project with Seedbed.

INTRODUCTION
A Personal Story

The Story Behind This Book

Every book has a story behind it—a story that answers the question, What led up to writing it down? The story behind this book unfolded in the wake of my recent retirement from a forty-year career as a seminary and university professor of Old Testament.[1]

Soon after my final semester of classroom teaching, I received two invitations to speak. The first called for giving a devotional at a gathering called "Awakening Project" held in Lexington, Kentucky, for "emerging adults and those who love them." For the second, I was invited by one of my former seminary students to come visit the church

---

1. I served on the faculty of Pentecostal Theological Seminary (1982–2007) and on the faculty of Lee University (2007–2022). I retired from full-time teaching at the end of the 2022 spring semester.

he pastored in Pennsylvania, and to deliver the Sunday-morning message on the anniversary of his tenth year as the senior pastor. As I prepared for both assignments, in light of the official end of my Old Testament teaching career, I was drawn to the end of the Old Testament, for the last two verses of the book of Malachi had long ago become life-defining Scripture for me. During my four decades of teaching, no passage of Scripture had more often, more directly, or more fully informed my sense of what I had been called to focus upon than this one:

> "Behold, I will send you Elijah the prophet
> Before the coming of the great and dreadful day
> 　　of the Lord.
> And he will turn
> The hearts of the fathers to the children,
> And the hearts of the children to their fathers,
> Lest I come and strike the earth with a curse."
> 　　(Mal. 4:5–6)

As I reviewed the entirety of Malachi 4 in preparing my thoughts, my focus narrowed down, like never before, to the single word, *"Behold!"* I noticed how this word introduced my life Scripture, and I also noticed that *behold* is also the word used to introduce the chapter's opening announcement—a statement that establishes the *context* of my life text:

> "For *behold*, the day is coming,
> Burning like an oven,
> And all the proud, yes, all who do wickedly will
> 　　be stubble.
> And the day which is coming shall burn them up,"

Says the LORD of hosts,
"That will leave them neither root nor branch.
But to you who fear My name
The Sun of Righteousness shall arise
With healing in His wings." (vv. 1–2a,
    emphasis added)

What caught my attention was how these two occurrences of the word *behold* in Malachi 4 were being spoken in order to command immediate attention, to turn a prediction of the future into an urgent imperative for the present, to get us *to see* something of immediate urgency that we are, no doubt, inclined *not to see*. This is the thought that gripped me as I prepared to make the move from this word of Scripture to the word I was to speak. It was a thought that gave me an entirely new angle on this ancient word of Scripture, which had long been a golden text for my life.

I had spent many years striving to get others to see the need and crucial importance of intergenerational reconciliation and relationship. But now all that striving and teaching and praying and waiting and working to get people, especially young people, to see this was suddenly being overtaken by an overwhelming sense that it was now time to shout, *"Behold!"* *"Behold*, the day is coming! And *Behold*, God is sending the prophet to turn hearts before the coming day!" It all seemed a bit like the time when Jesus said to his disciples in John 4:35, "Do you not say, 'There are still four months and then comes the harvest'? *Behold*, I say to you, lift up your eyes and look at the fields, for they are already white for harvest!" (emphasis added).

So I went both to the gathering in Lexington and later to the church in Pennsylvania, carrying something more than an expository lesson on Malachi 4. I had the sense that I was to issue an imperative, to call God's people to behold what was right now before our eyes. It was not a call to look *for* something, but rather to open our eyes and to look *at* something that is already right in front of us: *the coming day of the Lord!* We can see the day of global pandemic and its fallout that has not yet stopped falling. We can see the day of national divisions so deep as to raise questions about the very survival of our nation. We can see the day of disruption in global economics to the point of unsettling the entire world order. We can see the day of military upheaval so great as to threaten a new world war. We can see all this about *our day*, but can we not see *the day of the Lord*?

God calls it "the day when I act" in Malachi 4:3 (ESV), and in verse 5, God calls it "the great and dreadful day of the Lord!"[2] Perhaps that is why we have such a hard

---

2. The phrase, "the day is coming," in Malachi 4:1 needs some explanation. It appears frequently in the Bible's prophetic literature to speak of eschatology or "last things." Sometimes it is simply rendered "that day" (Isa. 2:20; 4:2; 7:18–23; 12:4; Jer. 4:9; Amos 8:9; 9:11; Mic. 7:11–12; Zeph. 3:16; Zech. 12–14; Matt. 24:36; Mark 13:32; Luke 21:34–35; 2 Tim. 1:12). Throughout Scripture it appears to be the most succinct way of referring to the end time, the time when God finally intervenes and acts to set all things right. In fact, God himself comes close to defining "the day" this very way when he calls it "the day when I act" (Mal. 4:3, as NIV and ESV translate it). Yet the most frequent and theologically established way of putting it is to call it "the day of the Lord," as the Malachi text does a few lines later in the

time seeing it. We are quite well-trained to suppress anything "dreadful" from appearing on the screens of our popular, consumer-friendly Christian faith, thanks to our diversions, our dismissals, and our denials. The word "dreadful" here in Malachi 4:5 is formed from the Hebrew term *yara*, "to fear." This very term is used three verses earlier when God affirmingly addresses "you who fear (*yara*) My name" (v. 2). This leads us to the crucial point: If we don't *fear* the LORD of the day, we won't *see* the day of the LORD. We will see only our days, which, just under the surface, are driven, dominated, and threatened to death by all our other fears—the fear of COVID, the fear of the other political party (whichever one threatens our own), the fear of economic collapse, the fear of intensifying natural disasters, the fear of mass shootings, the fear of the drug epidemic that's invading our communities and families, the fear of Russia and China and terrorists and whatever else appears in the handwriting on the wall that spells the prospect of our end.

---

expression, "that great and dreadful day of the LORD" (Mal. 4:5; cf. Isa. 2:11–12, 17, 20; 13:6, 9; Jer. 46:10; Ezek. 30:3; Joel 1:15; 2:1, 31; 3:14; Amos 5:18–20; Obad. 1:15; Micah 4:6; Zeph. 1:7, 14; Hag. 2:23; 1 Cor. 3:13; 5:5; 1 Thess. 5:2; 2 Thess. 2:2; 2 Peter 3:10, 12; Rev. 16:14). This day is "great" (Mal. 4:5), because, for those "who fear my name," God says, "the sun of righteousness shall rise with healing in its wings" (v. 2 ESV). This day is also "dreadful" (v. 5) because it is the day when "all that do wickedly" will be burned up (v. 3 DRB). But God's people have shown a perennial tendency to resist facing the "dreadful" part until its visibility is all but lost in our vision and in our version of the faith (see, for example, Amos 5:18–20).

However, for those who fear the Lord of the Day, something else is written: the promise of a saving sunrise ascending from the midst of this present darkness (v. 2). This promise is hinged on two turning points. First, there is the move of turning to Scripture, as God says in verse 4, "Remember the Law [Torah] of Moses." And then at last, there is the beholding of God's prophetic move to turn hearts—a turning of the old to the young and of the young to the old, a move to redress what is arguably the greatest social malignancy of our day, which would indicate why it would be the Lord's top priority before the great and dreadful day of the Lord.

This is the thrust of the message that I first shared at the meeting in Lexington and then delivered to the church in Pennsylvania. But in that second speaking engagement I added one final point. This additional point took the form of one more call to "Behold!" For this I turned to the story in Luke 1 that picks up where Malachi leaves off. Here the angel Gabriel meets Zechariah the priest beside the altar in the Jerusalem temple. Gabriel bears the message that Zechariah and his wife, Elizabeth, were soon to have a child in their old age. This child would be a son named John, who would be raised up "in the spirit and power of Elijah, 'to turn the hearts of the fathers to the children,' and the disobedient to the wisdom of the just, to make ready a people prepared for the Lord" (Luke 1:17). However, Zechariah pushes back, saying, "How shall I know this? For I am an old man, and my wife is advanced in years" (v. 18 ESV). Gabriel then responds by saying, "*Behold*, you will be mute and not able to speak until the day these things take place" (v. 20, emphasis added). As a friend of mine pointed out, here we can see how the shutting down of one human capacity (speaking) has the effect of heightening another human capacity (beholding), as it certainly did in Zechariah's case, as the story in Luke 1 goes on to show. For Zechariah did not have to wait even one more day to begin beholding the fulfilment of his son's heart-turning mission. The turning of his own heart to his son had already begun. And it was only the beginning—the sunrise of a new day (cf. Luke 1:78). Indeed, it marked the coming, the dawning of the day of the LORD.

When I came to the end of this message on that Sunday morning in Pennsylvania, I was suddenly struck by an impulse to do something that I had not previously planned. I looked over the front edge of the pulpit at the pastor who was sitting on the front row and asked him if he would be okay with my doing something rather out of the ordinary and spontaneous. And, of course, he was quick to indulge me and give a thumbs-up to his old professor. I then looked out over the congregation and said, "I would like every *old* person here to come forward to the altar." I let that statement hang there in all its unflattering boldness and brazenness, without any attempt to soften its blunt force.

What happened in the next few moments was amazing and revelatory. First, there was stunned silence, followed by glances of one to another, giving way to chuckles, and then squirming in the seats. Finally, people began to leave their seats and come forward until a line stretched across the front of the church from wall to wall. Without realizing or anticipating it beforehand, I had just posed, in a way more effective than I ever could have imagined, one of the great psychological and spiritual struggles of our day—the struggle of facing and coming to terms with our old age. It is not a small struggle in a culture like ours that has made old age synonymous with irrelevance, outdatedness, obsolescence, and, above all, the subject for jokes, as can easily be seen wherever birthday cards are sold.

Yet here these brave souls now stood at the altar, like Zechariah in the biblical story I had just read to them. Standing there in a bald admission of their old age, they had every reason, just like Zechariah, to see themselves as too old—too old to be the bearer of life-giving newness that could make an abundance of difference in our broken world. But this was a pregnant moment, and as I and the church pastors prayed over these spiritual fathers and spiritual mothers, I believe all of us standing there could hear more than ever before the call to "Behold!" "*Behold*, the Day is coming! *Behold*, God is sending forth His message before the coming Day to turn our hearts, from the oldest to the youngest! *Behold*, God is determined to enable us to behold this, even if He must *dis*able us to do so!"

As I went back home after my weekend in Pennsylvania, reflecting on that Sunday morning service, it occurred to me that the message I had delivered there was more than a message for the day or the week. It seemed more like the mission for this remaining season of my life. I told someone that I felt a bit like Paul Revere must have felt when he took his midnight ride. I was gripped by the desire to ride through the land and sound a wake-up call to anyone who has ears to hear, to anyone who would dare to listen, to anyone who would wake up and behold, especially anyone in the ranks of the older generation. It is a desire that has not left me, and it has led to, among other things, the decision to write this book. This is the desire at the heart of this book—a book that I hope and pray will serve God's own desire, His determined, passionate, relentless, and unstoppable desire to bring about the turning of our hearts.

The Rest of the Story

Alongside the decision to write this book came more specific decisions about how I would write it. First, I wanted to write things my children and grandchildren might one day want to read. As I thought about them, I began to write down a list of bullet points that, for me, had become crucially relevant to the intergenerational heart-to-heart message of Malachi 4. These points fell out as follows:

- Tell stories to your children when they are young.
  - And tell them with all your heart!
  - Tell them as if their lives depended upon it—
  - Because they do!
  - Remember that children's hearts are hardwired for stories!
- Listen to your children's stories when they are coming of age.
  - And listen with all your heart!
  - Listen as if your life with them depended upon it—
  - Because it does!

- Tell stories that include your weak points.
  - Your weak points can form the strongest links with your children.
  - Your weak points can become stronger than your power points.
  - Weak points of your stories and theirs form the deepest bonds.
- Tell your stories to your questioning children.
  - When they question you about your rules:
  - Their questions are often signals of readiness to hear your stories.
  - Their questions are often *not* a sign of rebellion.
  - So answer them by telling them your stories with all your heart!
  - Tell them as if their lives depended upon it—
  - Because they do!
  - Tell them the weak points of your stories that led to your rules.
  - Tell them how your weak points led you to see how God rules!
  - Tell them as if God were the main character in your stories—
  - Because He is!
  - And use the term "us" when you tell them your stories.
  - Do this as if your children were included in the "us"—
  - Because they are!
- Know there is a promise as you include your children in your stories.
  - They will become a part of your stories.

- – And you will become a part of their stories.
    - – These will become stories they will tell their children.
    - – And you will become protagonists in their stories.
    - – You will avoid being antagonists who are cut out of their stories.
    - – And your stories and their stories won't drive you apart.
    - – They will instead draw you together.
    - – Your hearts and their hearts will be turned toward one another.
    - – Your hearts and their hearts will be turned toward God.
- Know that God is ever turned toward all of us.
    - – God is a Father whose heart is ever turned toward His children.
    - – He turns His heart to us through the stories He tells us.
    - – These stories are writ large in Scripture in the Torah and Gospels.
    - – And God's own Son is the author and finisher of the ultimate story.
    - – This is the story that finally and fully includes us all!

I ventured a few days later to share these points with my two grown daughters, Emily and Hannah.[3] Emily's

---

3. Emily Moore Young, my firstborn, is married to Matthew Young, and they live in North Carolina with their three children: Evan, Emmett, and Anna Margaret. Emily has a BA degree in English from Lee University and a MA degree in English literature from Wake Forest University. In addition to raising her

initial response was that this could very well serve as an outline for a book. And I responded by suggesting that this might be a book that the two of them could help me write. Then Hannah added her affirmation of the idea, but with an unintentionally humbling twist. She said, "Dad, I suspect more people will read this book than anything you have ever written." One could only hope. In any event, what came together for me in that moment was a clearer sense of *what* needs to be written, *how* it needs to be written, *when* and *why* it needs to be written, and *to whom* it needs to be written. So here is how this project first began to come into focus for me:

- **What needs to be written?**
  - A book on how the hearts of elders need to be turned to their children.
- **How does it need to be written?**
  - By turning to my own children to keep me focused on the heart of my intended audience and even to seek their help in the writing of this book.
- **When and why does it need to be written?**
  - Right now, because the heart gap between elders and their children has never been more gaping and urgent, to the point of posing disastrous prospects.

---

children, she teaches English literature at a Christian school and does freelance copyediting for scholarly publications. Hannah Elizabeth Moore has a BA degree in history from Lee University. She is a motivational speaker and blogger, and she serves in her local congregation as a member of the creative preaching team and as a worshipper in the sanctuary choir.

- ***To whom does it need to be written?***
  - To "as many as the LORD our God shall call"[4] and is already calling (!) to be parents and spiritual elders and mentors to the multitudes of insufficiently parented children of the rising generation in the context of our own families and extended families and in the context of the church, the household of faith.

Overview of Content

What this book is about can now be elaborated a bit further by offering a brief overview of how the content of this project has finally taken shape in the seven chapters of this book.

Introduction: A Personal Story

In this introduction I am presenting the personal story that brought me to the point of writing this book. Along with sketching the content of each chapter, I am attempting to describe my motivation, purpose, and intended audience. This introduction intends to show how a lifelong focus on the heart-to-heart connection between generations, as envisioned in Malachi 4:5–6, has become a matter of fresh vision and urgency for me and, I believe, for us all, convincing me that the time is right for this study on spiritual parenting.

---

4. I use the words here from Peter at the end of his message on the day of Pentecost in Acts 2:39 (KJV).

Chapter 1: The Biblical Roots of Spiritual Parenting

In this chapter I begin with the recognition that spiritual parenting goes down to something as deep within us as our very origin in the image of God. From this starting point, I proceed to offer a biblical and theological grounding for spiritual parenting. I point out how, from the beginning of the book of Genesis, God is presented as the first and the ultimate Parent. God's first act of parenting is to bestow parental blessing, and I show how blessing from this point forward becomes a major theme of Genesis and a primary practice and responsibility of spiritual parenting in God's covenant with His people. I trace the growing theme of God as Father in the Old Testament and how it comes into full display through God's own Son in the New Testament. The divine glory of the Father-Son relationship, as seen especially in the story of the Mount of Transfiguration, is shown to be a revelation of God's gracious will to restore broken relationships in the human family, especially those most toxic of broken relationships, those between earthly fathers and their sons.

Chapter 2: Telling Stories to Our Children

This chapter highlights the simple and undeniable truth that children have been made to hear and to love stories. I show how the early books of the Bible, along with other passages of Scripture, repeatedly emphasize the responsibility of parents to respond to this innate interest in their children by telling them the stories that transmit God's covenant faith from generation to generation. I include a personal testimony of how the seriousness and sacredness of this practice with little children became for me a life-changing revelation, which has deeply impacted my view of spiritual parenting.

Chapter 3: Listening to Our Children When They Are Coming of Age

This chapter addresses the important place in spiritual parenting of listening to our children, particularly when they become emerging adults. I discuss how the Genesis story of Jacob and Joseph provides a model narrative in Scripture that yields significant insights on this key practice of spiritual parenting. So much of this practice involves how God works in our hearts over long stretches of time to sow and to cultivate divinely inspired blessings meant to be given to our children. I share several personal stories of how these truths have come home to me in the raising and blessing of my daughters.

Chapter 4: Telling Our Stories to Our Questioning Children

This chapter focuses upon Moses's role as a biblical prototype of spiritual parenting and his explicit instruction on the practice of it. The discussion focuses upon how Moses instructs the new generation of the children of Israel in the book of Deuteronomy, especially in chapter 6. This biblical passage includes Israel's greatest commandment (i.e., the Shema); a depiction of the expanding impact of transmitting the covenant faith (from heart, to home, to city, to nation); and an anticipated parental opportunity that shows the vital importance of drawing our children into the sacred story whenever they begin to question the ethical commitments of their elders. I proceed to show how Scripture promotes telling our questioning children our own personal God-stories as well as the canonized God-stories of Scripture. Our personal God-stories are the ones that follow the scriptural pattern of revealing both our weaknesses and God's overcoming strength in our lives. I introduce this chapter with a brief testimony illustrating practical application.

Chapter 5: Our Weak Points Turned into Strong Links

This chapter focuses upon the story and figure of Elijah, showing how this prophet, not unlike Moses, becomes a scriptural model and mediator of spiritual parenting. After reviewing Elijah's story in First and Second Kings, the discussion highlights how the weak points in Elijah's life become the turning points that bring him into his role of spiritual parenting and become the strong links of intergenerational relationship that connect Elijah to his prophetic and parental destiny and legacy. I then offer a personal testimony of how the truths highlighted in Elijah's story first took root in me. This chapter concludes with a homily written by my daughter Hannah—a fitting conclusion to this chapter's emphasis upon how God's strength is made perfect in weakness.

Chapter 6: The Spirit of Spiritual Parenting

This final chapter has a complementary relationship with chapter 1. Together these two chapters form a biblical and theological frame. The first chapter highlights the biblical roots of spiritual parenting, grounded in the life of the heavenly Father and His only begotten Son. This concluding chapter proceeds to show Scripture's emphasis on the indispensable role of the Holy Spirit in producing the fruit of spiritual parenting. Attention will be given to the numerous ways that the two-volume writing of Luke-Acts presents the Holy Spirit's work in terms of restoring intergenerational relationships. This is shown in the nativity stories that begin Luke's Gospel as well as in the narrative of the outpouring of the Holy Spirit (near the beginning of the book of Acts). We will look finally at the Holy Spirit's work in and through Mary, the mother of Jesus—the spiritual parent above all others on earth. This book is fittingly capped off with a devotional that features a spiritual reflection upon Mary, written by my daughter Emily.

The Writing Approach

How I approached the writing of this book calls for further comment. Looking to my daughters, Emily and Hannah, to help me in the writing process was not only a means of writing the book but also a manifestation of its main message and end goal. It was a special opportunity for me to pursue the commitment of turning my own heart toward my children. It provided a chance for me to reflect together with them upon the stories we have lived and the stories we have shared with each other—including the good, the bad, and the not-so-pretty—and to draw from these stories some of the specific examples of the general truths that are here put forward. Emily and Hannah provided vital feedback to me during the writing process of each chapter.

This book also draws upon and features the personal stories and wisdom of others who have informed and inspired our lives through the years. Yet if this book has any general truths worth being put forward, then they must have grounding that is deeper than the background stories drawn either from our own personal lives or from the lives of others close to home. That deeper grounding must be found in Scripture.

Significantly, the Bible has much to say on the topic in view here. And drawing out key connections from the biblical witness is at the heart of the message and the method of this book. This will be pursued throughout the book, from the book's title, taken from Malachi 4:5–6, to the key points in every chapter. As we shall see, these key points have roots that grow from God's covenant life with His people in Genesis, the explicit exhortations and example of Moses in the book of Deuteronomy, the enduring example of Elijah in First and Second Kings, the message and mission of Jesus in the Gospels of the

New Testament, and the gift of the Holy Spirit poured into Mary, the mother of Jesus, and then poured out on all God's people in the book of Acts.

Timing, Purpose, and Audience

Finally, I want to focus on the *when* and *why* and the *to whom* of the writing of this book. As previously mentioned, Malachi 4:5–6 has been a life Scripture passage for me. It uplifts a vision of God's passion and promise for a heart-transforming work that will finally overcome the divisions between generations—divisions that otherwise have no other outcome and end than curse, as explicitly noted at the end of Malachi 4:6.

Throughout my adult life, at almost every turn, I have found myself coming under a burden, in one form or another, of the division between generations. This has been the case, whether in the context of my academic vocation, my local congregation, or my church denomination. What's more, the fractures have appeared even in the relationships much closer to home in my immediate and extended family. This has led me again and again to turn to Malachi 4:5–6, where I have come to find an undergirding promise and defining directive for my life. While both sides of the burden of intergenerational relationships have engaged me all along, it is understandable that my four-decade career as a teacher of college and seminary students has kept me primarily focused upon turning the hearts of the young to their elders. Although this focus has by no means come to an end for me, the beginning of this new season of my life has come with a fresh sense of vision and urgency for the elders' side of this intergenerational burden.

I pray this book can make a small contribution to beholding the mighty call and promise of God to turn the hearts of elders to their children before the great and dreadful day of the LORD. And may we live to see the awakening of an entire generation to the message and mission of spiritual parenting.

CHAPTER 1

THE BIBLICAL ROOTS OF SPIRITUAL PARENTING

So God created humankind in his own image;
in the image of God he created him:
male and female he created them.

God blessed them: God said to them, "Be fruitful,
multiply, fill the earth . . ."
God saw everything he had made, and indeed it was
very good.

—GEN. 1:27–28, 31A CJB

One of my earliest memories reaches back to a moment I had with my father when I was only four or five years old. I was standing beside him in the living room of our Michigan home, and we were both looking out the large picture window that faced our front yard. It was a cold, gray day, perhaps one of the first such days that signaled the end of fall and the beginning of winter. I was very concerned as I stood there beside my father. I had just come inside from playing in the yard, no doubt chased into the house by the windy chill in the air that day. The focus of my concern was a little flower I had just found growing in the grass near the edge of our yard. I told my father about the flower, and then I asked him, "Daddy, will the winter kill the little flower?" As the two of us stood there looking out the window and peering deeply into the long winter that lay ahead, my father said, "Son, don't worry at all about that. God will take care of that flower."

These words of my father have somehow survived all the many winters of my life. And to this very day, they stir to life something deep inside me that goes beyond any words I have to explain it. Yet I am inclined to think that the marvelous mystery of the impact of that childhood moment had something to do with the divinely designed life within every one of us humans—something that makes possible the connection of hearts between children, their parents, and God, something that can be conveyed by parental words that somehow relay the very Word of God.

I would suggest that what I have just described involves something that we never outgrow, something just as inherent and intrinsic to us in our old age as in our childhood. A recent moment in my life brought home this truth to me. My father died in 2010. He was eighty-eight years old. And, just the other day, almost a decade and a half after his death, the reach of his words crossed the barrier between his grave and my seventy-year-old life in this world. And I found myself once again, as it were, standing beside my father as that little boy looking out the picture window and hearing in the trace of his words the voice of the heavenly Father.

Here is how it took place. I have a Bible that was given to me by my mother when I was twelve years old, as indicated by my mother's handwritten words on the presentation page. This Bible went missing throughout most of my teenage years. It reappeared in my home after my father retired from his work at Ford Motor Company. As I came to discover, my father had taken this Bible to the factory where he worked and kept it there for years, reading it during his break times. On many pages I found pencil and pen marks, which seemed to indicate my father's attempt to keep track of his place in his reading-through-the-Bible efforts. Date references indicated as much. By the time my father brought this Bible back home, its cover had become extremely worn, so I sent it to a bindery where it was fitted with a new hardback cover. Since that time, this Bible has become increasingly valuable to me, especially because of the traces of my dad left behind by his marks on its pages.

Now that he is gone, I sometimes open this Bible to some verse I happen to be studying to see if my father left any mark beside that particular verse. One day last week I was reading the exodus story and came to the verse that spoke of how the mother of the infant Moses, before hiding him from Pharoah's execution order, "saw that he was a beautiful child" (Ex. 2:2). I found myself wondering whether that verse stood out to my father, because, if it did, then perhaps it was because I stood out to my father in a way not unlike Moses did to his mother. So I looked up the verse in my re-bound Bible, but I found no mark beside it. I then remembered that this Exodus verse was referenced in the faith chapter of Hebrews 11. When I thumbed through that Bible and came to Hebrews 11, I found a page that was almost completely unmarked except for a bracket around one verse, specifically verse 23a, which reads: "By faith Moses, when he was born, was hid three months of his parents, because they saw he was a proper child" (KJV).

How is it that a seventy-year-old man like me can still find himself looking for (and finding!) a fresh word of approval from his long-deceased father? Again, I would submit that it has to do with something that reaches down to the very core of our nature and identity as human beings, indeed, something that reaches all the way back to God's own word of approval, His "very good" (Gen. 1:31), when He created humans in His own image in the beginning.

I am pointing to these experiences in my own life to prompt you, my reader, to consider such experiences in *your* life. These are the kinds of experiences that I see play out repeatedly in the PBS television program, *Finding Your Roots*. Each episode of the show goes something like this. The host, Henry Louis Gates Jr., and the members of his team invite a celebrity to appear as a guest on the show after they have done extensive research on the guest's genealogical records. As significant storylines of distant and previously unknown ancestors are unearthed and shared with the guest, moments of deep emotional response, even tears, suddenly overtake the guest in a way that the guest is at a complete loss to explain. This happens again and again on the episodes of this show. I believe this attests to something deep within our human core that relates to our inherent need and proclivity for parental connection beyond what is merely biological. And I believe Scripture offers us a far more credible way of finding the roots of this aspect of our humanity than anything offered by evolutionary biology or secular anthropology.

So, what I will attempt to do in the remainder of this chapter is to consider the biblical foundations of the spiritual aspect of parenting. Perhaps a better designation would be the scriptural root system of spiritual parenting. This gives us a more dynamic picture of what nourishes our spiritual parenting, makes it grow, and gives it life in the first place.

God as First Parent

Spiritual parenting begins with God. And we can see this from the very beginning of Scripture, right after we see the Spirit of God moving over the chaotic waters of creation in the Bible's first verses (Gen. 1:1–2). Genesis is a fitting title for this biblical book of beginnings. It presents the origins of many things, including the origins of spiritual parenting. This can be seen on Scripture's very first page.

Here we see God acting not only as Creator and King but also as the first Parent, the original and ultimate Parent. We know God acts as *Creator* here by creating the universe and everything in it (vv. 1–31). God also acts as a *King* by commanding things to come about (vv. 3, 6, 9, 11, 14, etc.); indeed, "God said . . . and it was so." As a King, God exercises dominion and even delegates some of that dominion to humans (vv. 26, 28). But God can also be seen here taking on the role of a *Parent*—a role that is played out even more dramatically in Genesis 2 in the intimate details of how God gives birth to human beings (vv. 7, 21–23). He forms and brings them into being through close and direct contact with His own being. This is why the prophet Isaiah could look back and connect God's role as Creator with His role as Father:

> But now, O LORD,
> You are our Father;
> We are the clay, and You our potter;
> And all we are the work of Your hand. (Isa. 64:8)

Genesis 1 reinforces this thought by showing God as the source of not only creation but also procreation. He gives plants and animals the powers to reproduce "after their kind" (vv. 11–12, 24–25 NASB). But when God makes man and woman, He makes them in His own "image" and "likeness" (vv. 26–27). In effect, God makes humans uniquely after *His* own kind. He then gives them the procreative mandate to become parents themselves, to "multiply, and fill the earth" (v. 28 NASB). By so doing, they will extend God's image and likeness, including *His parenting role* (see Gen. 5:1–3), from generation to generation.[5]

---

5. The term "generations" (*toledot* in the Hebrew) even becomes a major theme through the rest of the book of Genesis by its use in the repeated phrase, "these are the generations of [so and so]," which subsequently introduces almost every other major section

Blessing as the Primary Practice
of Spiritual Parenting

Yet there is nothing in Genesis 1 that points to God's parenting role with humans more directly than the initial action He takes after creating them. As Scripture simply and plainly puts it, "God blessed them" (v. 28). From this point forward "blessing" (from the Hebrew verb *barak*) becomes one of the most prominent terms and themes in the rest of the book of Genesis (9:1). Notice how this theme is emphasized at the pivotal point of the book (12:1–3), when God turns His attention from bringing forth the whole world (vv. 1–11) to bringing forth His chosen people (vv. 12–50):

> Now the LORD had said to Abram:
> "Get out of your country,
> From your family
> And from your father's house,
> To a land that I will show you.
> I will make you a great nation;
> I will *bless* you
> And make your name great;
> And you shall be a *blessing*.
> I will *bless* those who *bless* you,
> And I will curse him who curses you;
> And in you all the families of the earth shall be
>   *blessed*." (Gen. 12:1–3, emphasis added)

____

of the book (Gen. 2:4; 5:1; 6:9; 10:1; 11:10, 27; 25:12, 19; 36:1, 9; 37:2). *Toledot* is a noun formed from the verbal root *yalad*, which means "to beget" or "to give birth."

God blesses the humans He brings forth in Genesis 1. In like manner, human parents thereafter in Genesis bless the children they bring forth (4:1; 5:29; 9:26–27). And this is clearly the most significant and defining interaction that takes place between parents and their children throughout this book of beginnings. This is highlighted by all the drama that unfolds in and around the act of blessing in episode after episode. For example:

- When Isaac approaches the end of his life and blesses his twin sons, Jacob and Esau, as each of them struggles against the other to get the greater blessing (27; 28:1–4).
- When Jacob, nearing his own death, blesses Joseph's sons and gives priority to the younger son over the firstborn, against Joseph's expressed wishes (48).
- When Jacob (a.k.a. Israel) blesses each of his twelve sons as a culminating act of his life and a capstone to the overall structure of the book of Genesis and the parental theme that is presented throughout (49).

In this way, Genesis shows the blessing of one's children to be a primary concern and responsibility of parents and the crowning act that highlights the spiritual dimension of parenting.

The Meaning and Significance of Blessing from the Beginning Until Now

More will be said about blessing in subsequent chapters. At this point, I would simply note that the term *blessing* can cover a wide range of usage in Scripture, just like it does in our contemporary usage of the term. It can refer to common words of affirmation and well-wishing (e.g., Ruth 2:4; Matt. 5:44) as well as to solemn pronouncements reserved for the holiest of moments, such as wedding ceremonies (Ps. 45:2), royal coronations (1 Kings 2:45), or deathbed farewells (Gen. 27:1–4). But I would suggest the following working definition of blessing that could cover this entire range: *Blessing is all about sharing words with our loved ones that speak to the deep significance of their identity and their destiny.*[6] And it all begins with our Father in heaven blessing us, His human offspring, with blessings that empower us as humans, made in God's own likeness, to be a source of blessing. This is blessing that is meant to flow forward, first from us as parents to our children and then outward to the ever-widening scope of relationships that ultimately reach to "all the families of the earth." This ultimate outreach is explicitly emphasized, as noted, in the blessing of God upon Abraham (Gen. 12:1–3), whose very name means "father of many nations."

This is clearly what God intended from the beginning of time. However, the great curse of our time is that this call, this responsibility, this authorization to be a source

---

6. As I like to put it, blessing is all about "words that go with the grain of life." This thought of "going with the grain of life" is meant to highlight how words of blessing align with the specific life bent of the one being blessed (speaking to identity), while also serving to generate the fruitful fulfillment of that person's life (speaking to destiny).

of blessing has been largely and increasingly lost, particularly in the parent-child relationship. And this is the case not just out there among the families of the world but also much closer to home, in the families within the household of faith, the family of God. Where blessing is absent, curse is present. For curse is the opposite of blessing. And absence of blessing in the parent-child relationship is undoubtedly the curse that's in view for the time of the end, as declared by the prophet Malachi in the last words of the Old Testament:

> "Behold, I will send you Elijah the prophet
> before the coming of the great and dreadful day
>   of the Lord.
> And he will turn
> The hearts of fathers to their children,
> And the hearts of children to their fathers,
> Lest I come and strike the earth with a curse."
>   (Mal. 4:5–6)

So God makes blessing a primary responsibility and priority of parenting from the beginning. However, we now find ourselves in a culture that, to say the least, has lost sight of the primacy of blessing. It is not hard to find parents who feel responsible for being the source for their children's food, shelter, clothing, and making sure they get a good education. However, parents' attention to being the primary source of speaking life-generating blessing into the hearts of their children has become harder and harder to find. Even in the church, this has become, to a large extent, a lost practice. And this loss will not be rectified by all the discipleship in the world that's conceived only in terms of putting Bible knowledge into the heads of our children.

As long ago as 1986, this point about the loss of the blessing was made with compelling conviction and urgency to the evangelical church in America by family counselors Gary Smalley and John Trent in their book, *The Blessing*.[7] This book was filled with sound biblical teaching on the blessing; keen, clinically supported insight into the widespread brokenness in families where the blessing is lacking; and much practical wisdom on how the practice of blessing can be recovered and revived in our families and in our churches. These authors wrote insightful chapters on each of the five important elements they saw in the biblical practice of the blessing:

- Meaningful Touch
- A Spoken Message
- Attaching "High Value" to the One Being Blessed
- Picturing a Special Future for the One Being Blessed
- An Active Commitment to Fulfill the Blessing[8]

As relevant as this wise message on the blessing was when it was first published in 1986, I would say that it is far more relevant and urgent today. My purpose here is not to rehearse its message but only to heartily endorse and commend it to anyone wanting further elaboration on the concept of blessing and guidance on how it can be put into practice.

---

7. Gary Smalley and John Trent, *The Blessing* (Thomas Nelson, 1986).

8. See this summary by Smalley and Trent, *The Blessing*, 26–33.

The Revelation of God as Father
in the Old Testament

Yet the burden of this chapter is to highlight something that goes deeper than the how-to of blessing. As noted, we first need to recognize that God, as the ultimate Parent of us all, is the ultimate source of all the blessing that would flow from us to our children. This gives our spiritual parenting, with its primary focal point in the blessing of our children, a divine grounding and well-spring that lies deeper than our own human know-how. So, if our spiritual parenting is to succeed in the lives of our children here on earth, it will find its source in the headwaters of the blessing of our heavenly Father.

Alongside the unfolding theme of parental blessing in the narrative of Genesis is the theme of the naming of one's offspring. Once again, this is a parental act and responsibility that appears first with God. In Genesis 1:26, God says, "Let Us make [*Adam*] in Our image, according to Our likeness" (NASB). This is an act of naming as well as creating, according to Genesis 5:2, where we see the convergence of God's act of creating, blessing, and naming: "Male and female created he them; and blessed them, and called their name Adam, in the day when they were created" (KJV). Hereafter we see an emphasis in Genesis on human parents exercising this responsibility to name their offspring.[9] As in the case of parental blessing, naming plays a key role in defining a child's identity. And God, who exercises His parental

---

9. Gen. 4:25–26; 5:3; 16:11, 15; 21:3–6; 25:24–26; 29:32–35; 30:4–13, 17–24; 35:18; 41:50–52.

role in naming humankind in the first place, continues to take up this parental role on those special occasions when He *re*names Abram to Abraham (17:1–6), Sarai to Sarah (17:15); and Jacob to Israel (32:28; 35:10).

In these moments of divine renaming, God is redefining the identity and the destiny not only of a person but also of an entire people. This is why Isaiah the prophet can look back on these Genesis moments and declare, "Thus says the LORD, who created you, O Jacob, And who formed you, O Israel: 'Fear not, for I have redeemed you; I have called you by your name; You are Mine'" (Isa. 43:1; see also 45:3–4).[10] God's parental emphasis upon the names and the naming of His children has obvious implications for how seriously we as parents should take the names and the naming of our own children. What's more, it should have implications for how seriously we should take the names of any son or daughter, who just might be in need of our blessing or even our spiritual parenting.

In my own experience in spiritual parenting, I could not even begin to count the number of times I have seen God's Word reach deeply into the heart of a young person by playing on the meaning of his or her name. It's no wonder, really. For what could possibly reach more deeply into the heart of a son or a daughter than the realization that God is calling them by name and thereby

---

10. See also Isaiah 51:1–2, where God says, "Look to the rock from which you were hewn, and to the quarry from which you were dug. Look to Abraham your father and to Sarah who bore you; for he was but one when I called him, that I might bless him and multiply him" (ESV).

naming the significance of their origin or the promise of their destiny? We see numerous examples of this in Scripture,[11] but nowhere more prominently than in the stories of Genesis.[12] And the specific stories of God's naming Abraham (17:1–5) and Israel (32:24–32) provide examples not only of how God does this for individuals but also of how God is committed to doing this corporately for all his people and ultimately for the blessing of "all the families of the earth" (12:1–3).

The stories of Genesis, then, provide the foundational revelation of God as Father. Yet it is worth noting that God's role as Father came into much clearer focus for His people in the Old Testament through two defining events in their history. These events were the exodus from Egypt and the return from Babylonian exile. Here is what Moses says when he reflects on the exodus in Deuteronomy 1:

> "The LORD your God, who goes before you, He will fight for you, according to all He did for you in Egypt before your eyes, and in the wilderness where you saw how the LORD your God carried you, as a man carries his son, in all the

---

11. Examples include Moses (Ex. 3:4); Samuel, whose name means "God heard" (1 Sam. 3:10–18); Ezekiel, whose name means "God hardens," and is told by God, "I have made your face hard against their faces" (Ezek. 3:8 NRSV), using the same verb that appears in Ezekiel's name; Zechariah (Luke 1:13); Mary (vv. 30–33); Peter (Matt. 16:18); and Saul (Acts 26:14).
12. Examples include Sarah (Gen. 17:15–16), Isaac (vv. 17–19), and Hagar (21:17), as well as Abraham (17:1–5) and Jacob/ Israel (32:24–32).

way that you went until you came to this place."
(vv. 30–31)

And here is what the prophet Isaiah says in his prayer for those he foresaw coming home from Babylonian captivity in Isaiah 63 and 64:

> Doubtless You are our Father,
> Though Abraham was ignorant of us,
> And Israel does not acknowledge us.
> You, O Lord, are our Father;
> Our Redeemer from Everlasting is Your
>   name. (63:16)

> But now, O Lord,
> You are our Father;
> We are the clay, and You our potter;
> And all we are the work of Your hand. (64:8)

The Revelation of God the Son
in the New Testament

It was only with the coming of Jesus, though, that God as Father came into full view. The revelation of the Son brought with it the revelation of the Father. Or, said differently, as the Father revealed the Son, the Son revealed the Father. We hear Jesus himself repeatedly making this point in the Gospel of John. We hear it when Philip asks Him, "'Lord, show us the Father, and we will be satisfied.' Jesus said to him, 'Have I been with you all this time, Philip, and you still do not know me? Whoever has seen me has seen the Father'" (John 14:8–9a NRSV). And He goes on to say, "Believe me when I say that I am in the

Father and the Father is in me" (John 14:11 NIV; see also 10:38). And then there is His statement to a group of Jews in the temple courts on one occasion: "I and the Father are one" (10:30 NIV). And on still another occasion Jesus tells another group of Jews, "Very truly I tell you, the Son can do nothing by himself; he can do only what he sees his Father doing, because whatever the Father does the Son also does" (5:19 NIV).

In all these references in the Gospel of John, we see Jesus pressing this emphasis. While this clearly has to do with establishing Jesus's uniquely divine identity, it also has to do with Jesus's new stress on God's identity as Father. While God's Fatherhood is present in the Old Testament, as we have noted, Jesus lifted this revelation to an altogether new height, moving it from a somewhat rare motif in the Old Testament to a major emphasis in the story and message of Jesus in the New Testament.[13]

This emphasis appears in full force at the baptism of Jesus when, as the Gospel of Luke records, "the Holy Spirit descended in bodily form like a dove upon Him, and a voice came from heaven which said, 'You are My beloved Son; in You I am well pleased'" (Luke 3:22). In this moment we see the supreme example of the Father bestowing the blessing on His Son.

---

13. It comes as a surprise to most people that explicit references to God as Father appear only about two dozen times in the Old Testament while appearing hundreds of times in the New Testament. There is nothing in the words of Jesus in the New Testament Gospels that receives more emphasis than God's identity as Father.

In the Sermon on the Mount in Matthew's Gospel, Jesus references God as "Father" no less than seventeen times. And all these references bring attention to more than just *the fact* of God's identity as Father. They also draw attention to *the kind* of Father that God is, and how this models the kind of parenting God expects from us. We see this when Jesus says, "Be perfect, therefore, as your heavenly Father is perfect" (Matt. 5:48 NIV), and again when He says, "If you then, being evil, know how to give good gifts to your children, how much more will your Father who is in heaven give good things to those who ask Him!" (7:11).

Yet the most emphatic way that Jesus gave primacy to God's identity and nature as Father is when, in response to His disciples' request to teach them how to pray, He says, "In this manner, therefore, pray: *Our Father* in heaven, Hallowed be Your name" (Matt. 6:9, emphasis added; cf. Luke 11:2). Jesus was teaching His disciples to follow His own pattern of making "Father" the primary way of approaching and addressing God.

Much more could be said about the enormous amount of emphasis on God as Father in the New Testament. There is Jesus's parable of the prodigal son, and His most famous statement, "For God so loved the world that He gave His only begotten Son" (John 3:16). And we remember the last words of Jesus on the cross: "Father, 'into Your hands I commit My spirit'" (Luke 23:46), and then the last words of Jesus before His ascension: "Go therefore and make disciples of all the nations, baptizing them in the name of the Father and of the Son and of the Holy Spirit" (Matt. 28:19). While there are many other important ways that God's identity is presented in the New Testament, including such ways as King, Judge, Shepherd, Redeemer, and Creator, there is none given such preeminence by Jesus as this.

The apostle Paul, in Romans 8, sees the Holy Spirit making the revelation of God's Fatherhood come alive in the innermost being of believers. As Paul puts it: "You received the Spirit of adoption by whom we cry out, 'Abba, Father.' The Spirit Himself bears witness with our spirit that we are children of God, and if children, then heirs—heirs of God and joint heirs with Christ" (vv. 15b–17a). This important truth would seem to be precisely in line with how Jesus identifies the anticipated gift of the Holy Spirit. He calls it "the Promise of My Father" (Luke 24:49). This arcs back to Jesus's words in Luke 11:13: "If you then, being evil, know how to give good gifts to your children, how much more will your heavenly Father give the Holy Spirit to those who ask Him!" The Spirit, then, comes as a Fatherly promise, about which Peter can say on the day of Pentecost, "The promise is for you and your children and for all who are far off—for all whom the Lord our God will call" (Acts 2:39 NIV).

The Glory of the Divine Father and Son and the Brokenness of Human Fathers and Sons

In our gender-sensitive day and age, some have questioned whether all this New Testament emphasis upon God's identity as Father and Son has had the effect of privileging male identity over female identity. This question gets posed in the following way. Given the fact that Genesis 1:27 clearly indicates that God's image in humans is manifest from the beginning in their being created "male *and female*" and given the additional fact that, in a few instances, Scripture does feature passages where God is presented in female terms,[14] why is there all this culminating emphasis on the male terms for God's identity?

Of course, none of us can presume to know all the reasons why God chose to reveal Himself the way He did. Yet here is a thought worth considering: Could it be that God revealed Himself in terms of Father and Son not because these terms represent the most privileged terms, but rather because they represent (indeed *re*-present!) what has tragically become most broken in the human family? In other words, could it be that the revelation of the heavenly Father through the Son by the Holy Spirit in the New Testament includes a direct answer to the broken connection between *earthly* fathers and their sons, as highlighted in the final verse of the Old Testament?[15] For it is revealed there that the crying

---

14. Psalm 123:2–3; 131:2; Deuteronomy 32:18; Isaiah 42:14; 49:15; 66:13; Matthew 23:37; Luke 13:34; 15:8–10.

15. There are those who might struggle with my suggestion here, thinking it falls short of seeing the revelation of God the Father and Son as being rooted deeply enough in the eternal being of God's nature. To those having this reservation, I would simply say that I lean heavily here on the word of the apostle Peter, speaking of God the Son in 1 Peter 1:20—"He was foreknown before the foundation of the world but was made manifest [or revealed] in the last times for the *sake of you*" (ESV). I am no philosophical theologian, but it seems quite clear to me that the issue here

need leading up to the end of time, indeed, "before the coming of the great and dreadful day of the LORD," is for the divided and disconnected hearts of fathers and sons to be turned back toward one another (Mal. 4:5–6).[16]

---

concerns time and eternity, how God's being in eternity relates to how God comes to be revealed in time. I see this statement in 1 Peter 1:20 rooting the identity of God the Son in the very nature of God's being in eternity, while recognizing the revelation of God the Son as occurring in time, specifically "in the last times" and "for the sake of you," that is, for the sake of all of us believers, past and present, who are being addressed by the apostle Peter's words. That is how I am seeing my proposal above that God has revealed God's self to us as the heavenly Father and Son "in the last times" (indeed, in the New Testament times; cf. Heb. 1:1–3), and that God has done so intentionally "for the sake of [us]," indeed for the sake of addressing our brokenness, which would include and provide remedy (indeed, eternally efficacious and timely remedy before "the great and dreadful day of the LORD") for the particular brokenness between earthly fathers and sons, specified as a particular and crucial focus of God's concern at the end of our Old Testament Scripture.

16. The point I make here entails reading the Malachi 4:6 reference to "fathers" and "sons" in a gender-specific way, according to the specific gender of the Hebrew terms. Yet I realize that these masculine nouns in the Hebrew can also be read in a gender-inclusive way and rendered "parents" and "children," as seen in such translations as the NIV, NRSV, CEV, and CEB. I would suggest that the context of Malachi 4 provides support for both readings by appealing to two ancestral fathers of Israel— namely, Moses and Elijah. First, comes the call in Malachi 4:4 to "remember the Law [Torah] of Moses," who is known for leading the "children ('sons' used in its gender-inclusive sense) of Israel" (e.g., Ex. 3:10). Then comes the call in Malachi 4:5–6 to "behold" God's promise to send Elijah, who is known for becoming a

Leading up to this ending, Malachi 4 names two fathers who are especially known for raising up spiritual sons. Moses, who is mentioned in verse 4, is known for raising up Joshua. And Elijah, who is mentioned in verse 5, is known for raising up Elisha. In subsequent chapters, we will be taking a closer look at both Moses and Elijah as key biblical models of the restoration of spiritual parenting.

Yet these two earthly fathers, at best, are merely forerunners of the Father-Son restoration that unfolds in the coming of Jesus. And nowhere is this specific restoration shown more clearly and fully than in the transfiguration story. Here we find these same two earthly fathers, Moses and Elijah, appearing on a mountain with Jesus, along with Peter, James, and John (Matt. 17:1–8; Mark 9:2–8; Luke 9:28–36). These three disciples behold Jesus transfigured into a form of brilliant radiance, and then they witness Moses and Elijah, who lived many generations earlier, now talking with Jesus. The Gospel of Luke records that these ancestral fathers talk with Jesus about the "departure [or 'exodus'], which He was about to accomplish at Jerusalem" (9:31 NASB). As supernaturally amazing as this appearance of Moses and Elijah is, it is quickly surpassed when a cloud engulfs them all and a voice comes out of the cloud, saying, "This is My

------

"father" to the "sons [used in its gender-specific sense] of the prophets" (e.g., 2 Kings 2:7–12). When it comes to our own day and time, I would suggest that our prisons are filled with the tragic and overwhelming evidence that the relational brokenness between fathers and their sons is a gender-specific malady without parallel in our social world.

beloved Son. Hear Him!" (v. 35). The cloud then lifts, and the disciples see Jesus all alone.

What makes the Father-Son import of this text so significant is its context. All three Gospel accounts introduce this event by specifying that it occurred about one week after Jesus informed the disciples that He would be going to Jerusalem and there suffer rejection and execution at the hands of "the elders, chief priests, and scribes."[17] This means that the transfiguration event takes place in direct relation to Jesus's acknowledgment that He is about to face complete and fatal rejection by the present elders of Israel. But on the Mount of Transfiguration, two *past elders of Israel* are divinely sent to be present with Jesus and to speak to Him about this very ordeal that He is facing and making known to His disciples. And these two elders from the past are not just any elders. As I like to put it, they are first-string elders. Moses and Elijah are the two elders of ancient Israel most known for their fathering role of raising up spiritual sons as successors. Just think of it. Even Jesus, as "the Son of Man,"[18] needed earthly elders to meet with Him before His meeting with the Jerusalem elders who would reject Him and execute His departure.

---

17. See Matthew 16:21; Mark 8:31; and Luke 9:22. Matthew and Mark specify the time as "six days" later (Matt. 17:1; Mark 9:2), and Luke, less specifically, says, "about eight days" later (9:28).
18. This is how Jesus identifies Himself to the disciples when He informs them of His forthcoming rejection by the elders in Jerusalem (Luke 9:22).

Jesus is about to be *taken down* by the elders of His time, but in direct counterpoint to this, He is *taken up* into the presence of two of the greatest elders of all time! Yet that is not all. This is only a segue to take everyone on that mountain into an even higher revelation of a Father-to-Son and Son-to-Father connection. "This is My beloved Son," sounds the voice of the heavenly Father from the midst of the cloud, "Listen to him!" (Luke 9:35 ESV). In this crucial moment of Jesus's mission on earth we see a divine revelation linking earthly fathers (Moses and Elijah) with the heavenly Father in the life of the Son. It reveals that what earthly fathers have in their power to bestow on their spiritual descendants can somehow be connected to what the heavenly Father wills to bestow on His beloved Son and all those who would now listen to Him.

The Restoration Coming Down from the Mount of Transfiguration

Where does the story go from here after Jesus and those three disciples come down from the mountain? All three Gospel accounts of the transfiguration are immediately followed by an account of a desperate father who brings his afflicted son to Jesus (Matt. 17:14–21; Mark 9:14–29; Luke 9:37–42). The father explains to Jesus that his son is often seized by a spirit that causes this child to inflict self-harm, trying to drown him or throw him into a fire. The father tells Jesus that he had first brought his son to Jesus's disciples, but they were unable to cast out the spirit. Jesus responds by expressing exasperation with

the entire generation, "O faithless and perverse generation, how long shall I be with you and bear with you?
Bring your son here" (Luke 9:41; see also Matt. 17:17
and Mark 9:19). Then Jesus proceeds to heal the son. As
the Gospel of Luke records: "Then Jesus rebuked the
unclean spirit, healed the child, and gave him back to his
father" (9:42).

Coming immediately after the Father-Son revelation on the Mount of Transfiguration, this story of
a desperate father bringing his afflicted son to Jesus
would seem to be inherently related to what had just
occurred on the mountain. There the heavenly Father
brings a transfiguring revelation to His beloved Son,
who then comes down the mountain and brings a transforming restoration of a son to his father. And Jesus's
restoring work here is clearly shown to involve far more
than this one individual father and his son. The disciples
are being brought into this work by the previous words
of the heavenly Father: "Listen to him!" (Matt. 17:5 ESV;
Mark 9:7 ESV; Luke 9:35 ESV). And then come the next
words of Jesus that address His entire generation: "O
faithless generation" (Mark 9:19). And then come the
words of Jesus to the disciples when they ask, "Why
couldn't we cast out the evil spirit?" It is "because of
your unbelief [or faithlessness]," comes Jesus's reply
(Matt. 17:20). This is the same issue Jesus raises with
the desperate father: "If you can believe, all things are
possible to him who believes." To which the father replies,
"Lord, I believe; help my unbelief!" (Mark 9:23–24). And
it is the same issue Jesus raises with the entire generation when He first responds to the father by exclaiming,

"O faithless generation" (Mark 9:19; see also Matt. 17:17; Luke 9:41).

The Father in heaven has sent the Son to restore the faith to a faithless generation, to restore the faith to all generations, from generation to generation, from father to son, from parents to their children. And at the turning point in this mighty move from transfiguration to restoration we hear the cry of a desperate father, a helpless parent, who cries out to Jesus for help. His cry can well represent all of us who carry the burden of spiritual parenting. "Lord! Help my child!" But this cry to Jesus, at Jesus's prodding, leads to another cry: "Help my unbelief!"

This father's encounter with Jesus leads all of us to what is doubtless the key to all spiritual parenting. It is none other than crying out and listening to Jesus. In other words, the key is fervent prayer, "prayer and fasting," as Jesus finally tells His disciples at the end of this episode (Matt. 17:21; Mark 9:29). This is heart-turning prayer to the one from whom all blessings flow; indeed, the one who is the source of all spiritual parenting.

Summary

If you are reading this book, perhaps it is because you are sensing your own need for help in the practice of spiritual parenting. It might be a need involving some perceived lack, whether in the parenting you have received or in the parenting you feel you now have or do not have to give. This need might concern either your own flesh-and-blood children or spiritual sons and daughters beyond your immediate family. In any case, this chapter has pointed to the ultimate source and root system where help for this need is to be found.

God's Word shows us how important spiritual parenting is to God, and how important this unfolding revelation from God's Word is to spiritual parenting. God is the Father of us all (Mal. 2:10). We have noted how He has shown His own parental commitment and example to us from the beginning by creating us in His own image, naming us, and blessing us. We noted how He bestowed upon us these parallel capacities and responsibilities in the procreating, naming, and blessing of our children from generation to generation. We saw how God called Abraham to extend this parental calling and endowment through his own family by being a "father of many nations" (Gen. 17:5) and thereby bringing blessing to "all the families of the earth" (12:1–3). We observed how God carried this blessing forward in and through the people of Israel, despite their flaws, failures, and setbacks. And through the pivotal events of the exodus from Egypt and the exile in Babylon, we saw how God renewed and further revealed His identity as Father. But most importantly of all, we acknowledged how God addressed the deepest aspect of our need when it comes to spiritual parenting. And that is the need for the hearts of elders and children to be turned once again toward one another, to heal all our generation gaps, especially those separating fathers from sons and sons from fathers. The heavenly Father has given the definitive remedy by sending His own Son, so that the Son could reveal the Father and impart to us "the promise of the Father" (Acts 1:4 KJV), who now says to us, "Listen to him!" (Luke 9:35 ESV).

The following chapters will provide further help from God's Word on spiritual parenting. Yet all that follows should be seen as stemming from the grounding revelation that we have surveyed here in this chapter. As we listen further to the Word of God, we should do so knowing that the God of the Word is the beginning and end of all spiritual parenting.

CHAPTER 2

TELLING STORIES TO OUR CHILDREN

Listen, my people, to my teaching;
turn your ears to the words from my mouth.
I will speak to you in parables
and explain mysteries from days of old.

The things which we have heard and known,
and which our fathers told us
we will not hide from their descendants;
we will tell the generation to come
the praises of [the Lord] and his strength,
the wonders that he has performed.

He raised up a testimony in [Jacob]
and established a Torah in Isra'el.
He commanded our ancestors
to make this known to their children,
so that the next generation would know it,
the children not yet born,
who would themselves arise
and tell their own children,

who could then put their confidence in God,
not forgetting God's deeds,
but obeying his [commandments].

—Ps. 78:1–7 CJB

"For what great nation is there that has God so near to it, as the Lord our God is to us, for whatever reason we may call upon Him? And what great nation is there that has such statutes and righteous judgments as are in all this law [Torah] which I set before you this day? Only take heed to yourself, and diligently keep yourself, lest you forget the things [plural of *davar*] your eyes have seen, and lest they depart from your heart all the days of your life. And teach them to your children and your grandchildren. . ."

—Deut. 4:7–9

Jesus said, "Let the little children come to me and do not hinder them, for to such belongs the kingdom of heaven."

—Matt. 19:14 ESV

A Parable for God's People

Taking my cue from the quotation from Psalm 78, I will open this chapter with a parable. It goes like this:

When God was looking for a people to call His own, He went to all the peoples of the world and asked them what they would do if He became their God and they became His people.

He asked the Greeks, "If I become Your God and you become My people, what will you do for Me?"

The Greeks said, "Master of the universe, if You become our God and we become Your people, we will create for You the most beautiful works of art and the most profound systems of philosophy the world has ever known. All people will come and worship You because of Your beauty and Your wisdom."

And God said, "Thank you." And He went on.

And God went to the Romans and He asked them, "If I become Your God and you become My people, what will you do for Me?"

The Romans said, "Almighty God, if You become our God and we become Your people, we will set Your standard at the head of our armies and we'll put Your banner before the caravans and fleets of our commercial empire. All people will come and bow down before You because of Your power and Your might.

And God said, "Thank you." And He went on.

God went to all the peoples of the world and got their offers. Finally, He came to a scrawny bunch of nomads in the desert called Hebrews. Now these nomads were shrewd traders. And God said to them, "If I become your God and you become My people, what will you do for Me?"

And they said, "Lord God, we cannot offer You great works of art or systems of philosophy; it is not within our capability. Nor can we offer

You great power or wealth; You can see our poor herds and tents. But, if You become our God and we become Your people, we will tell the stories of Your deeds to our children, and they to their children, and they to their children to all generations.

And God said, "It's a deal."[19]

This little parable highlights a priority that stands at the very heart of biblical faith and practice: the telling of stories by one generation to the next is God's prime means of propagating and perpetuating the faith of His people. The Scriptures quoted point to this priority and bear witness to its gravity and necessity for every generation.

A Biblical Pattern of Storytelling from Generation to Generation

We see the priority Scripture places on storytelling in Exodus, the foundational salvation story of Scripture. As this narrative unfolds, God provides a means within the story itself for this story to be remembered and recounted throughout all generations. It is as if the story cannot wait until the end to address this crucial concern. It comes in the account of the Passover feast,

---

19. My source for this parable was a paper presented at the annual meeting of the Society for Pentecostal Studies in 1985 by Michael B. Dowd, entitled "Contours of a Narrative Pentecostal Theology and Practice."

presented as both a part of the story and an initiating instance of what will thereafter be an annual occasion for the story to be told again and again. And especially significant is the way children are given a prime place and role in this interaction:

> "So this day shall be to you a memorial; and you shall keep it as a feast to the LORD throughout your generations. . . .
>
> "And it shall be, when your children say to you, 'What do you mean by this service?' that you shall say, 'It is the Passover sacrifice of the LORD, who passed over the houses of the children of Israel in Egypt when He struck the Egyptians and delivered our households.'" So the people bowed their heads and worshiped. (Ex. 12:14a, 26–27)

This same pattern of child-focused storytelling appears repeatedly in the first books of Scripture:

> And you shall tell your son in that day, saying . . . (Ex. 13:8)

> So it shall be, when your son asks you in time to come, saying, "What is this?" that you shall say to him . . . (Ex. 13:14)

> "When your son asks you in time to come, saying, 'What is the meaning of the testimonies, the statutes, and the judgments which the LORD our God has commanded you?' then you shall say to your son . . ." (Deut. 6:20–21a)

"This may be a sign among you when your children ask in time to come, saying, 'What do these stones mean to you?' Then you shall answer them . . ." (Josh. 4:6–7a)

"When your children ask their fathers in time to come, saying, 'What are these stones?' then you shall let your children know, saying . . ." (Josh. 4:21–22a)

These passages clearly show that children, their questions, and their strategic role as receivers of the story were, from the outset, to be taken with utmost seriousness by God's people. And this set up a scenario that banked upon two trusted assumptions: children would ask questions, and children would be ready to hear stories. Can anyone who has ever had children or cared for small children doubt the truth of these two things? It is as if children come preloaded with a proclivity to ask questions about everything and also with an appetite to hear stories, as if they had been hardwired for them. God's covenant with His people took advantage of these two aspects of the nature of children. And we would do well to do the same.

The Story that Preserves Our Life and Our Children

Psalm 78 calls God's people to "tell the next generation the praiseworthy deeds of the Lord" (vv. 4–5 NIV). And the psalm itself does this too! It presents a poetic retelling of the overarching story of God's people from their exodus from Egypt (v. 12) to the establishment of David's kingship (vv. 70–72). As the psalm unfolds, it makes clear that the life, the very survival of God's people, is at stake in the faithful keeping and passing down of this story. Much of the psalm emphasizes times in the past when many of God's people lost sight of this story and perished along the way (vv. 31–33). These times become dark chapters that are incorporated into the story. Yet this only adds urgency to the foundational covenant obligation that the older generation make known to their children the "testimony" and "law [torah]" that God established in Israel (v. 5).

Torah, although often translated "law," is much more than a legal document. As a term that becomes the very title of the Bible's first five books, Torah is essentially a story. To be sure, it presents the text of the law with its many commandments, but all in the context and framework of a story. Indeed, it is the foundational portion of the God-given story upon which the life of God's people, and ultimately all people, depends (see Gen. 12:1–3).

Like Psalm 78, the Torah itself emphasizes the dire consequences, both potential and actual, that come when God's people fail to preserve and keep true to their own story. And so the story recounts how unfaithful Israelites perish in the wilderness (Exodus 32) and how an entire generation is consigned to wait, wander, and die outside the promised land (Numbers). This story and the responsibility of each successive generation to carry it forward to the next generation continue throughout the rest of the Old Testament and into the New.

As Matthew 19:14 shows us, Jesus gave primary-age children a primary place in His kingdom mission and message. It is obvious that Jesus is here reflecting the priorities of the Hebrew faith and practice in which He Himself had been raised. These priorities are highlighted in the other Scripture passages previously quoted (Psalm 78 and Exodus 12). The story in Luke 2:41–52, which tells how the twelve-year-old Jesus astounded the temple teachers in Jerusalem with His engagement of the Scriptures, gives us a small but revealing glimpse into this faith practice that undoubtedly characterized and shaped Jesus's own childhood. All of this points unmistakably to the fact that God's Word takes children and their intergenerational participation in the faith community with extreme seriousness.

Taking Children Seriously

This truth was pressed home to me in an unforgettable way many years ago on a particular Sunday morning at my local church. My wife and I were about to enter the sanctuary when a friend who worked in the children's department approached us, somewhat frantically, asking if we could step in and take care of the three-year-old children as a last-minute replacement for a teacher who had to leave. Feeling a bit on-the-spot and ill-prepared, we agreed, and our two daughters, who were in grade school then, were eager to come along with us for the adventure.

When we entered the classroom, about a dozen three-year-olds were already bouncing off the walls, and a frazzled assistant worker said, "Great! I'll go to the church kitchen and get the apple juice and vanilla wafers that we've prepared." I thought, *Good! This will give us time to think of a game plan.* When the trays of refreshments came through the door, the children quickly sat down and calmed down to enjoy their sweet treats served by my wife and daughters. And I used this time to configure the remaining chairs into a circle in the play area of the room. I soon began to call the children to come and sit in the circle, so that I could tell them a Bible story, which I was hoping would quickly come to mind.

All the children found a seat in the circle, except one. A little boy had run into a small wooden playhouse in the room and wouldn't come out. I asked the children, "Who's in the playhouse?"

And they said "Adam!"

Then I said, "Adam is hiding!" It was as if I had been handed a cue, and I began telling the children the Bible story about another Adam who was hiding—hiding in a garden, afraid because he had disobeyed (Gen. 3).

As I elaborated this point of the Bible story, another little boy across from me erupted with a big sneeze, which suddenly yielded, let's say, a major nose issue. With the help of one of my daughters, I soon had a tissue in hand as well as another teachable moment. I was getting the boy's nose cleaned up, asking him to blow extra hard into the tissue, when I thought to ask the children, "Did you ever notice that sometimes you need the help of another person to get your own nose cleaned or to get other parts of your body clean?" The little children began to nod their heads in agreement. I then asked the little boy with the freshly cleaned nose, "What's your name?" And I promise you he said, "Wesley." I couldn't help myself. I was prompted to dip, ever so briefly, into a bit of church history, telling these three-year-old children that, long ago, there was a man named Wesley who helped all of God's people to see how much we needed one another's help to get clean and to stay clean, and how that it's often the yucky stuff on the inside, and not just the outside, where we need the most help to get cleaned up.

This led me to think of another Bible story that had to do with this very thing—the story of Jesus washing the feet of His disciples and showing them how they needed to help one another get clean and stay clean (John 13). And it occurred to me in that moment that a very effective way to teach this story to these three-year-old children was for me to wash their little feet. Soon we got help retrieving from the church kitchen a huge cooking pot with several inches of water in the bottom. I learned that day that, if you need to captivate the attention of a group of three-year-olds, use water! They all stood around the pot and took turns reaching down and feeling the water and filling up little cups and then pouring them back out into the pot. Then I announced that I was going to wash the feet of each one of them, just like Jesus washed the feet of His disciples. The pot was just big enough to allow each child in turn to get into the pot and then sit down on the rim.

As soon as they realized the liturgical procedure, there was a burst of raised hands and voices shouting, "I want to be first, I want to be first!" I responded by telling them that the disciples of Jesus were saying the very same thing on the night when He washed their feet (Luke 22:24ff.). At that moment I looked at my two daughters and said, "What happens at our house when one of you starts shouting, 'I want to be first?'"

Hannah declared the answer like it was a commandment from Sinai: "If you try to be first, then you have to be last."

That's right, "If you try to be first, then you have to be last," I repeated. But now who should have nestled up beside me in the chair right next to me but Adam, who looked up at me with the sweetest expression and with the sweetest tone said, "But I want to be last." And this was enough to prompt my announcement that, because Adam wants to be last, he gets to be first. My wife, Jean, who tends to be more discerning at detecting the Adamic nature in people and especially in children, still thinks to this day that Adam was duping me. In any case, I proceeded to wash Adam's feet, and then I washed the feet of all the other children one at a time as they respectfully and respectively took their turns.

When I was finishing with the last child, the classroom door opened, and we were told that the church service was about to end and our time was almost up. I turned to the children, and exclaimed, "Time is almost up! We need to clean up the church! Yes, time is almost up! We need to clean up the church!" (see Rom. 13:11–14). Then the children began to help me pick up all the toys that previously had been scattered all around the room. It was amazing to see how this little platoon of three-year-olds pitched in and put things back in place. One little girl at one point ran over to me and said, "What can I do?"

I looked down beside where I was standing and saw a little baby doll, without any clothes, lying on the floor. I picked up the doll, and lifted it up before all the children, saying, "Should this baby be lying on the floor like this?" And that same little girl then reached up eagerly to receive the doll. She then found a blanket, in which she carefully wrapped the baby before placing it in a cradle.

When we came to our final moments together, the room was back in its original good order, except for the pot in the middle of the floor. I walked over to it and then declared to the children, "It's time to get the dirt out of the church!" I picked up the pot, which still held the foot-washing water, carried it over to a window, opened the window, and then poured out all the contents on the ground below, as I repeatedly chanted the words, "It's time to get the dirt out of the church!"

Soon all the children were picked up by their parents and caregivers, and my family and I went home to enjoy our Sunday afternoon. Not until later that day, when I had the chance to settle down and reflect on this experience, did its import and impact fully hit me. I was a seminary professor, but I realized that I had just experienced the greatest inspiration to teach that I had ever known. And with that realization I was immediately struck by a thought that came to me as a message from God. It tenderly touched my heart and sharply pierced it, all at the same time. Although this occurred over three decades ago, the deep impression it made has never left me. It occurs to me now that, until this very moment, I have never written it down, but here it is: "The apple juice and vanilla wafers served to these children were as precious in the eyes of God as the Communion wafers and grape juice served on that day in the church sanctuary." From that day forward, I was never again able to relegate the teaching of children to mere babysitting or to some endeavor of less significance than what I practiced in my seminary and university classrooms. I was never again able to shake this conviction: God takes children and our responsibility to tell them the stories of our faith with holy, awesome seriousness . . . and we should too.

CHAPTER 3

LISTENING TO OUR CHILDREN WHEN THEY ARE COMING OF AGE

These are the generations of Jacob.

Joseph, being seventeen years old, was pasturing the flock with his brothers. . . .

Now Joseph had a dream, and when he told it to his brothers they hated him. . . .

Then he dreamed another dream and told it to his brothers and said, . . . "Behold, the sun, the moon, and eleven stars were bowing down to me." But when he told it to his father and to his brothers, his father rebuked him and said to him, "What is this dream that you have dreamed? Shall I and your mother and your brothers indeed come to bow ourselves down to the ground before you?" And his brothers were jealous of him, but his father kept the saying in mind.

—Gen. 37:2a, 5, 9–11 ESV

The Story of Jacob and Joseph

When it comes to spiritual parenting, the importance of listening to our children when they are coming of age cannot be overestimated. This is clearly depicted in what is no doubt a model narrative found early on in our Bibles—namely, the story of Jacob and Joseph. Its lesson on listening can apply to the parenting of our own biological children, but also more generally to the parenting of spiritual daughters and sons in the context of intergenerational relationships.

The story of Joseph in the book of Genesis begins with an introductory phrase, "These are the generations of Jacob" (37:2a ESV). Parallels of this phrase are used repeatedly throughout Genesis to mark the beginning of major sections of the book. "These are the generations of [X]" appears in 2:4; 5:1; 6:9; 10:1; 11:10, 27; 25:12, 19; 36:1, 9; and 37:2. The Hebrew term translated "generations" is *toledoth*, and some translators believe that a preferable rendering of the phrase would be "this is the story (or account or history) of [X]." This rendering appears in more than a few translations (see NABRE, NIV, NLT, GNT, CEV). In any case, this introductory phrase draws attention to what is surely one of the most prominent features and formative factors of the first book of our Bible: God's Word to us from the beginning comes through stories that bind the generations together.

This introductory phrase in Genesis 37, together with what follows, clearly reflects this concern for the passing of stories from the older generation to the younger generation. But we are also shown how crucial it can be for the older generation to pay attention to the stories of the younger generation. For these stories can unfold to become the main storyline going forward for the old as well as for the young.

Accordingly, what gets announced as "the story . . . of Jacob" (Gen. 37:2a NRSV) promptly turns to the story of Joseph (37:2b). Joseph's story then unfolds to become the longest continuous narrative in the entire book of Genesis (37–50). It all begins with Joseph telling his brothers and father about some dreams he had. This sets off a sharp reaction of resentment and rebuke against Joseph. Yet amid this pointed push-back, coming first from his brothers and then from his father, there appears a very significant counterpoint. It comes in the statement, "but his father kept the saying in mind" (37:11b ESV). With the including of this little detail, we are alerted to a tension within Jacob. Despite finding his son's words offensive and objectionable, Jacob nevertheless cannot bring himself simply to cast them off. He finds himself taking them to heart, even while outwardly dismissing them. This strain in the relationship between Jacob and Joseph represents an intergenerational tension that is not unique to this story. It is found universally as a recurring pattern that appears again and again as each generation encounters and interacts with the next.

We are talking about that phase in life when our children start telling us things that are not mere echoes of what we have told them and taught them to say. It is that moment when we are confronted and often stunned by the realization that our kids have a mind of their own.

Their coming of age can be an unwelcomed and intrusive reminder that we ourselves are aging. Note how the Joseph story begins with a reference to his being seventeen years of age. It is an age when our kids can suddenly surprise us with the revelation that they have dreams for themselves that are not the same or even in accord with the dreams we have for them. This is when the conversation between us and our children can break down.

Notice how the conversation between Joseph and Jacob comes to an abrupt halt with Jacob's contesting and testy questions to Joseph (v. 10). That's the way it is quite often when our children are coming of age. The conversation comes to an impasse, and neither parent nor child can see any way forward. Both are at a loss in knowing how to keep the conversation going. This often happens in the parent-child relationships in a family, but it can also happen corporately in the breakdown of relationship and interaction between generations in a local church congregation or a denomination or in a community or even in an entire nation or international culture. Remember the 1960s? And, what's more, what about today?

Although Jacob did not keep the conversation going, he at least "kept the saying in mind" (v. 11b ESV). In other words, Jacob kept thinking about what Joseph told him, that is, the story of his dreams. This phrase, "kept the saying in mind," in the Hebrew consists of only two words, a verb (*shamar*) that connotes "observing" or "watching" and a noun (*davar*) most often translated simply as "word." Jacob watched over the word! We get the idea here of Jacob giving sustained attention to what his son had told him, continuing to hold onto it and to ponder it.

We can be reminded here of a striking parallel in the nativity story of Luke's Gospel when Mary responded to the story told by the shepherds on what was for them a holy night of angelic visitation and revelation. It had been a very different kind of night for Mary. Yet after the shepherds brought their uplifting report, "Mary," we are told, "kept all these things and pondered them in her heart" (Luke 2:19). Like her ancestral father, Jacob, so many generations before her, Mary had a son, but more than that, she had a word about her son—a word that was surely more than her mind could conceive. So she, like Jacob, kept the word in her heart.

In these parallel responses, both Mary and Jacob are, in effect, incubating what eventually turns out to be prophetic words that have everything to do with the identity and destiny of their children. Mary is no doubt doing this knowingly. After all, she had already received her own angelic revelation concerning her son (Luke 1:26–38), not to mention her miraculous conception! For Jacob, however, the word comes to him without any indication of its supernatural source. More often than not, this is the case for us. And this is what makes Jacob a particularly relevant model for us. Yet we should note that the examples of both Mary and Jacob surely reflect God's perennial desire to provide parents with insight into their children's divinely promised future. This is the divine desire and provision that leads to what Scripture repeatedly shows us to be the parents' most significant covenant interchange with their children: the blessing.

The Significance of Blessing in the Story of Jacob

As discussed previously in chapter 1, no theme in Genesis is more prominent than the blessing. Note the following points where this theme stands out:

- The entire narrative of Genesis culminates in acts of bestowing parental blessings:
  - Jacob blesses the sons of Joseph in Genesis 48.
  - Jacob blesses all twelve of his own sons in Genesis 49.
- The theme of blessing runs through the entire story of Jacob from the beginning:
  - First in relation to Jacob's birthright struggle with Esau in the womb (25:21–26).
  - Later in the birthright struggle between Jacob and Esau in the field (25:27–34), for the birthright determines which blessing each son is due to receive.
  - This plays out when Jacob tricks his dying father into giving him Esau's blessing (27:1–45).
- This sets up Jacob's pivotal struggle over the blessing:
  - Esau's anger over his lost blessing drives Jacob into an exile.
  - Yet in exile Jacob experiences such fulfillment of the blessing that it triggers jealousy and conflict with his father-in-law, Laban.
  - This conflict forces Jacob to return home and face Esau, whose blessing he had stolen many years earlier.
  - But on the way home, Jacob is forced to face even more: an all-night wrestling match with what he

comes to perceive as nothing less than the "face of God," prompting Jacob to declare to his mysterious divine assailant, "I will not let you go unless you bless me" (32:24–32 NLT).

So the story of Jacob has everything to do with his struggle to get the blessing and then finally to give the blessing to each of his twelve sons. And the transition from getting the blessing to giving it is not just a last-minute shift. It comes somehow in the long arc of the story of Jacob. And with his blessing upon Joseph in particular, it comes through words that are kept and watched over and pondered in his heart. As with Jacob, so with us, these words can come through wrestling and even wounding experiences. But as we see in the story of Jacob and Joseph, the words of a young person's dreams and a young person's story, kept in a parent's heart, can be the very seeds that germinate and finally bear the fruit of the parental blessing.

Jacob's Final Blessing Upon Joseph

Jacob's words of blessing spoken over Joseph at the end of Jacob's life point back to the beginning of Joseph's story. They point back specifically to those unwelcomed words Joseph spoke to his father concerning his dreams. Note Jacob's final blessing upon Joseph in Genesis 49:

Joseph is a fruitful bough,
    a fruitful bough by a spring;
    his branches run over the wall.

The archers fiercely attacked him,
    shot at him, and harassed him sorely;
yet his bow remained unmoved,
    his arms were made agile
by the hands of the Mighty One of Jacob
    (by the name of the Shepherd, the Rock of
    Israel),
by the God of your father who will help you,
    by God Almighty who will bless you
    with blessings of heaven above,
blessings of the deep that couches beneath,
    blessings of the breasts and of the womb.
The blessings of your father
    are mighty beyond the blessings of the
    eternal mountains,
    the bounties of the everlasting hills;
may they be on the head of Joseph,
    and on the brow of him who was separate
    from his brothers. (vv. 22–26 RSV)

The last verse of this blessing of Jacob upon Joseph forms a striking image of the fulfillment of what Joseph had dreamed so many years before as a young person coming of age. It was a dream that had seemed at the time to be ridiculously grandiose and preposterous—way too high-and-mighty to be believed. Yet, pondered and long incubated in the heart of the father, it now called for metaphors no less grand than "eternal mountains" and "everlasting hills" to represent its fulfillment. This is surely one of Scripture's most important lessons on how blessings can get sown and grown in the hearts of spiritual parents.

A Blessing for My Firstborn

During the first year of my four-decade teaching career, one of my seminary students asked me a question about these parental blessings that appear so prominently in the Pentateuch (Gen. 27; 48; 49; Deut. 33). I consider this one of the most important questions that was ever put to me by a student. He said, "Are these blessings wishes, prayers, or prophecies?" As a young professor, I didn't have an answer. I was completely stumped by the question. The answer came several months before I became a father, before my wife, Jean, and I experienced the birth of our firstborn child, Emily Jo.

Sometime between the student's question and Emily's arrival, my wife and I invited a seasoned missionary from Israel, Margaret Gaines to our home for dinner one evening. She had become legendary in our church circles by serving almost half a century in a small Arab village on Israel's West Bank, building a school for Arab children. After dinner, as we continued sitting at our table, Margaret told us stories about her life from childhood to the mission field. We were mesmerized by her stories, some of which we can still recall in vivid detail.

Margaret told one story of how her mother made for herself a place of daily prayer just inside the edge of the woods behind their rural Alabama farmhouse. Margaret as a very young child would try to sneak close enough to hear what her mother was praying. When her mother emerged from the woods with a sparkle in her eyes, Margaret would ask her, "Mama, what were you doing?"

And with a lift in her voice, she would reply, "I was talking to Jesus."

Margaret remembered how these words troubled her, for she thought, *If my mother is talking to Jesus, then Jesus might tell her that I have been stealing pickles from the pickle barrel at the back of the country store when I go there with my mother.*

In telling me this story, Margaret suddenly stopped and looked deeply into my eyes and said with a solemn fervency that still moves me, "Your intimacy with God will give you more authority with your children than anything else in this world." Those words were engraved on my heart that day, deeply enough to last a lifetime.

Near the end of our evening together, Margaret offered a prayer of blessing over our soon-coming child. I can't even begin to describe the sacred presence of that moment in our dining room. She prayed words I will never forget. Then several weeks later came the day when we brought our newborn Emily home from the hospital. Before entering our driveway, we stopped to collect our mail. It included a news magazine with a picture of an infant's face on the cover and a feature article inside surveying the latest science on early childhood development. When I later had the chance to read the article, I came to the final paragraph and its concluding line. It contained a verbatim match of the most memorable phrase in the prayer that Margaret had prayed over our soon-to-be-born child.

How could I see this as anything other than, to borrow Viktor Frankl's famous phrase, "a hint from

Heaven"?[20] For me, it was a word that I have kept in my heart for these last forty years. It is a word that carries and conveys the holy inheritance and promise of Emily's God-given life. It is a word that gave me the answer to my student's question about parental blessings: "Are these blessings wishes, prayers, or prophecies?" I came to the settled conviction that day that they can be all of the above or they can be altogether forfeited, depending upon the words that we keep or else fail to keep within our hearts.

This conviction springs from the even deeper conviction that when God gives us a child, God will give us the blessing that goes with that child. It is a transaction that turns on the heart, coming as a word conceived in the heart. It is a word to be kept and carried in the heart and not be aborted, a word that can grow and come to fruition across the span of a lifetime. And Scripture shows us how this word can come in all sorts of ways—ways that range from the supernaturally spectacular to the ever so subtle and mundane, from an angelic revelation, as with Zechariah and with Mary, to a mere "hint from Heaven" that shows up in our mailbox or in the prayer of a loved one or even in the unwelcomed words spoken by a child, like Joseph, at the point of his coming of age.

A Blessing for My Youngest Child

This latter type of scenario is more along the lines of what I have experienced with my second child, Hannah

---

20. Viktor Frankl, "Preface to the 1992 Edition," *Man's Search for Meaning* (Beacon Press, 2006), 112, Kindle.

Elizabeth. Allow me once again to share a personal story. I take the time to do this, because any wisdom in spiritual parenting that any of us have to give will begin in the heart and close to home before it can manifest in contexts beyond our own intimate circle.

Hannah was born ten weeks early, according to human reckoning. She spent the first month of her life in the hospital's neonatal care unit. The complications of her premature birth entailed a brain bleed on her third day of life. The damage of this brain bleed resulted in the diagnosis of spastic diplegia cerebral palsy, but my wife, Jean, and I did not receive this unwelcomed news until the day of Hannah's first-year checkup. We learned a lot about cerebral palsy in the following days and months. We learned about physical therapy and orthotic braces and crutches and walkers and developmental markers. Amid all of this, we learned that the extent of Hannah's brain injury could be determined only with time. What's more, through all this, my wife found her calling to become a nurse.

Despite the multitude of medical appointments for Hannah, there was much joy in her childhood. Although she was physically challenged, she was verbally gifted. She spoke her first complete sentence before she turned one and a half. Crawling across our living room floor with a children's storybook in hand, she said to me, "Read it to me." And she started singing almost before she started talking. "O Little Town of Bethlehem" was her first chosen anthem, which had to be sung with her mother every night for months on end. Without ever trying or realizing it, Hannah captured the spotlight of every room she entered with the brightness of her smile, the beauty of her blonde curls, and her articulate engagement with everyone around her. With complete obliviousness to her leg braces, crutches, and walker, Hannah could make everyone else forget them too.

As could be expected, the joys of Hannah's childhood provided no escape from the inevitable growing pains that would come with Hannah's coming of age. As her father, who was hoping and praying for the best for her, I was inclined to suppress any thought of the manifold struggles that lay ahead for Hannah and for our entire family. Jean, as her ever-vigilant mother, was always far ahead of me on that score. But there was one event in our family life that crashed in upon us all as a disturbing sign of the growing challenges that were eventually to come with Hannah's growing up.

When Emily was thirteen and Hannah was eleven, we were on a family vacation at the beach on the Gulf Coast, enjoying a time of respite together. We went to a fun restaurant one evening to have a family dinner. While sitting at our table we were suddenly interrupted when I was slammed from behind with a great force that shoved me into our table and almost knocked me out of my seat. It took only a second for me to realize what had happened. A grown man was now laying on his back on the floor beside me, looking up at me with the most pitiful and pleading expression on his face, pouring out an apology to me for having fallen on me.

His parents rushed across the restaurant to us and joined their son in effusively apologizing to me, while also tending to him and, with great exertion, helping him off the floor. I was trying my best to reassure them that I was entirely okay, for I could see all too clearly that this was an accidental fall by a young man with a disability much like Hannah's. The scene seized the attention of everyone in the restaurant for a minute until the commotion was quelled with no injuries reported, and happy restaurant noises resumed. But for me this brief break in the peace of our family vacation broke much more than that. As we drove back along the coast to our condo that night against the backdrop of the glistening ocean waves and darkening sky, I began to realize that the episode in the restaurant had broken my heart. I was feeling heartbreak for a family I did not know and, in the sudden light of that, heartbreak for my own family too. It was a realization I had never fully faced before. In that other family I had glimpsed something that seemed like a flash-forward to the future of my own family.

This sparked a penetrating reflection on the pain and the hope that resided deep in the heart of our family— the pain and the hope of past days, of the present day, and especially of potential days to come. It was as if we as a family, in a riveting moment of time, had been forced to face all this in the pleading face of that young man lying on his back on the floor of that restaurant. But if we had indeed been forced to face this, then the question seemed to be: "Is it time that we should talk about it?" As an Old Testament teacher, I couldn't escape the sense that this was a God-sent teachable moment. It was sent first to teach me something and then to give me something to teach. It was a lesson on the undeniable connection and indivisible unity of pain and hope and God and prayer.

I had taught my seminary students that the Lord's Prayer is the short answer to the disciples' question, "Lord, teach us to pray" (Luke 11:1), and that the book of Psalms is the long answer. It is a long answer because the book of Psalms both explores the heights of praise, elaborating "Hallowed be thy name" (Luke 11:2 KJV), and probes (in fully half of its contents!) the depths of lament, explicating "deliver us from evil" (v. 4 KJV). But I was now being taught a lesson myself about those depths and heights. And at the same time, I was being called to teach this lesson to our daughters, even at their tender ages.

What I was able to teach that night, in light of the human object lesson that God had allowed to crash into our dinner table, was this: "The Bible makes more room for our cries than we often can find in the church." God's Word makes room even when the church has suppressed lament for so long that it has forgotten how to lament. And if God makes room for our laments in Scripture's primary book of prayer, then God surely wants us to share our laments with Him and with each other, knowing that this will not *prevent* our praises but, instead, *vent* the very things that, when fully expressed, will propel our praises.

A Deeper Lesson from Deeper Listening

In time, this family experience, which happened more than twenty-five years ago, yielded an even deeper lesson for me. It is a lesson which brings me more directly to the focus of this chapter and one which I have begun to come to terms with only recently, even right up to the point of writing these words on this page right now. This lesson is all about how God has called me as Hannah's father to listen, truly and deeply listen, to what Hannah has been saying to me through her many laments throughout the years of her coming of age. I now see something far more clearly than I did at that earlier time. When that physically challenged, fully grown son fell into me and onto the floor of that restaurant that day, our family came face-to-face with the revelation that Hannah's cerebral palsy had floored us all. Ready or not, we had fallen into the midst of a life-consuming and life-defining struggle to rise up, so to speak, from that floor by trying to see Hannah rise up from that floor. For how else could we bear to see it? How else, but to cry out, "Dear God in heaven, I can't stand to see Hannah on that floor! There must be a way to see her rise up from that floor!"

So, for a very long time I have longed for the word that would see Hannah raised up, raised up from that low-down, God-forsaken floor of life—raised up to her full identity and destiny. And isn't this the kind of word that every daughter and son on earth most needs and wants from their parents, whether they know it or not? And isn't this the kind of word that every mother and father on earth most wants to bestow and bequeath to their child, whether they know it or not? Such a word, of course, is none other than the blessing. Yet what does it take for a father's longing and wish and prayer to bring forth the father's blessing? It would, no doubt, take hearing a word from the heavenly Father. And in my case with respect to Hannah, this has not come (at least not so far) by way of an angelic visitation. It has instead required me to listen, really listen, to Hannah.

So what could be difficult about that? From her earliest years, Hannah loved conversation, and I loved conversation. Hannah loved stories, and I loved stories. Hannah loved words, and I loved words. And all the special needs of Hannah's physical condition gave us far more than the average amount of opportunities for a father and daughter to walk and talk together along the path of life. I witnessed and experienced at close range Hannah's giftedness with words. And I saw how others in ever-widening circles also could see this as Hannah came of age. This even led to Hannah receiving some significant speaking opportunities along the way. It was easy for me, as someone who made his living with words, to latch onto the idea that speaking would surely be the arena of Hannah's primary calling in life and, thus, the primary focus of the parental blessing that I was to carry and, in the course of time, to convey to her. I held onto this thought so tenaciously and deeply in my heart that, without realizing it, I had a hard time hearing anything else. I had a hard time hearing Hannah.

I had a hard time hearing Hannah when she herself began to have a hard time hearing during her first year of college. In her case, it was quite literally a physical hearing problem due to extreme ear sensitivity that was somehow connected to her cerebral palsy. This forced her to resign from the college choir that she had dreamed of joining since she was a little girl, and it greatly curtailed her tolerance for even listening to music, whether recorded or live. I had a hard time hearing Hannah's lament as to the magnitude of this loss in her life. I had a hard time hearing how Hannah's loss of her song eventually took her down to places that veered dangerously close to the loss of her life. I had a hard time hearing Hannah when we took our walks together in our neighborhood and our talks seemed to click less and less and to grind more and more. I was trying hard to be the source of fatherly blessing that I wanted to be and that I had a reputation for being in the circles extending out from our home, but I had a hard time hearing Hannah's growing frustration with how I was not hearing her. She finally expressed it to me plainly, "Dad, I feel like you're not hearing me." These words cut like a knife. It was enough to generate my own frustration, but I somehow found the grace, like Jacob of old, to ponder Hannah's disturbing words in my heart.

My conversation with Hannah had come to an impasse, partly due to her hearing sensitivity and partly due to my hearing *in*sensitivity. It finally brought me to the place where all I knew to do was to admit that I didn't know what to do. It was a humbling admission for someone whose signature teaching had to do with the turning of the hearts of different generations toward one another. But here's where I know God intervened: He gave me the grace to overcome my pride and to admit this—even to Hannah.

What happened next was grace upon grace (and by the way, Hannah's name means "The LORD is gracious"). Hannah began to experience a noticeable decrease in her extreme hearing sensitivity. This happened around the time that one of her closest friends, whose name is Joy, suggested to Hannah that she might try coming to the church choir rehearsal just to see if she could stand it. Not only was Hannah able to stand it, in less than a month she was standing in the choir loft in our church sanctuary in our Sunday-morning worship services, singing with the church choir in full-throated and wholehearted praise to God. From that time until now, Hannah's worship has been sending rays of inspiration through the choir and congregation, especially among the many in our faith community who, for many years, have been fully and prayerfully cognizant of Hannah's struggles in body and soul. Hannah has her own story to tell about all this, and believe me when I say, I love hearing her tell it! One small part of her story is presented in her own voice at the end of chapter 5.

As Hannah likes to put it, God restored her song. And grace upon grace, God restored something at the heart of our conversation with one another. He remedied a disability in my own heart that had kept me from hearing something that Hannah had long been trying to tell me. I was able to see and to say to her that I had long imposed upon her my own bias that her primary calling was speaking, only to come lately to the realization that her primary vocation is worship. When I admitted and confessed this to Hannah, she thanked me for putting into words something that she had long felt but couldn't quite bring into focus. And soon afterward, in a time of personal prayer, the Lord brought something else into focus for me—sharp and piercing focus. It came in the form of a question to me: "Isn't worship your primary vocation too?"

This question has redefined my retirement. I have not retired from my primary vocation after all! And I now bear witness to this life-redefining revelation by standing on Sunday mornings when the choir stands to sing. I believe I have been called to join the choir, to join the choir from the congregation, to resist the temptation to be a mere spectator as I have been all too often and far too long. From now on I'm committed to resisting this temptation, for worship is indeed my primary vocation, not just on Sundays, but every day of every week of every year that I have left in my life on this earth. I want to stand up and answer my call to be a first responder. I want to rise up with Hannah. In accord with the words of the psalmist, "My foot stands on level ground; in the great congregation I will bless the LORD" (Ps. 26:12 RSV).

I have learned in the light of this experience that sometimes our hearts must be punctured and pierced in order to be turned—turned to the hearts of our children. And I have also learned that God, as the ultimate source of this heart-turning, sometimes discloses the grace and goal of it all—indeed, the holy word of parental blessing—only as we listen, truly listen, to our children and ponder their words in our hearts.

CHAPTER 4

TELLING OUR STORIES TO OUR QUESTIONING CHILDREN

"When your son asks you in time to come, 'What is the meaning of the testimonies and the statutes and the rules that the Lord our God has commanded you?' then you shall say to your son, 'We were Pharaoh's slaves in Egypt. And the Lord brought us out of Egypt with a mighty hand. And the Lord showed signs and wonders, great and grievous, against Egypt and against Pharaoh and all his household, before our eyes. And he brought us out from there, that he might bring us in and give us the land that he swore to give to our fathers. And the Lord commanded us to do all these statutes, to fear the Lord our God, for our good always, that he might preserve us alive, as we are this day. And it will be righteousness for us, if we are careful to do all this commandment before the Lord our God, as he has commanded us.'"

—Deut. 6:20–25 ESV

While I was in the middle of writing this book, I had a conversation with a friend, who asked me to describe to him what my book was about. After telling him that my book was about spiritual parenting, I spent some time giving him an overview of how I planned to address the topic. A few days later, we engaged in an email exchange, which I have copied and now added. I have done so with my friend's permission and with a few editorial changes to preserve anonymity and confidentiality. It occurred to me that this email exchange is a personal story that can offer a fitting illustration and real-life application of what I am attempting to bring forward in this chapter from God's Word, as given through Moses in the book of Deuteronomy.

Rickie,

My seventeen-year-old grandson and I went on a ten-hour road trip together. He is a Christian young man with a 3.9 GPA.

A few highlights of our conversation:

I said, "What about LGBTQ?"

He said, "I think everyone has the choice to choose what they want to be. However, I do believe that God created man and woman for marriage. I can see why people don't want to be Christians, because they are so mean!"

I said, "Why are you a Christian?"

He said, "I believe God sent His Son, Jesus, to die for my sin."

I said, "Why do you believe the Bible?"

He said, "I don't know."

He is being raised in a Christian home and will soon be a high school senior.

During college, he will step back from most of his parents' belief system and develop his own belief system. What will be the bedrock of his belief system?

How will your book relate to this scenario?

Sincerely, Joshua

Dear Joshua,

Thanks for sharing with me such a meaningful question—one that came from such a significant conversation between you and your grandson.

So, you ask, "How will your book relate to this scenario?" First, I think your exchange with your grandson finds a striking parallel in the scenario that Moses describes in Deuteronomy 6:20–25.

The last word in verse 20 is very significant. The son refers to a certain set of moral commitments in terms of what "the LORD our God has commanded *you*." He uses the pronoun "you" not "us," indicating that he is not owning these commandments but rather taking the first step of distancing himself from them and *dis*owning them, even though he hasn't yet taken the second step of disowning "the LORD *our* God." But Moses sees this whole scenario calling for the parent to recognize that it's time to tell the child the story that grounds the moral. This is the story that not only grounds the moral but also grounds the child. It is the story that provides the child with an identity, drawing him into the story, as indicated in the pronouns: "*we* were slaves"; "the LORD brought *us* out and gave *us* the land"; "the LORD commanded *us*"; "that *we* might always prosper and be kept alive."

This is the story that invites the child into the identity of the people who have been chosen by God and out of the enslaving identity of Pharoah's self-serving choice or even the false identity that comes from a source no deeper than one's own self-grounded choice, which is the false narrative that the world surrounding us right now is powerfully forcing and foisting upon us and our children. I see it in your grandson's statement, "I think everyone has the choice to choose what they want to be." It sounds like freedom, but it's bondage. It promises a sense of identity, but it yields a loss of identity. A loss of identity that is deep and detrimental enough to generate, especially in the young, a pandemic of anxiety, depression, and all kinds of questioning and experimenting with sexual identity, gender identity (e.g., with fabricated self-assigned pronouns), even species identity (e.g., with furries).

So in the light of Deuteronomy 6:20–25, I think the scenario with your grandson is a sign that he's ready to hear your faith stories, maybe even dying to hear them. And this is what my book is all about.

Moses as a Biblical Prototype of Spiritual Parenting

In this chapter, we will be focusing upon some scriptural wisdom on spiritual parenting that comes to us from the words of Moses. We observed in chapter 1 how Moses claims a special place in Scripture as a spiritual parent by the way he posthumously appears as an elder to Jesus on the Mount of Transfiguration (Matt. 17:1–8; Mark 9:2–8; Luke 9:28–36). When we consider the life and mission of Moses as it unfolds and develops in the Pentateuch, it is easy to see that Moses's role as a father to the children of Israel is an important dimension of his calling alongside his other roles, which include his being a prophet, a deliverer, a lawgiver, a judge, and a teacher. Moses's parental role comes to full development and expression in the last book of the Pentateuch, Deuteronomy. Here he becomes nothing less than a biblical prototype of spiritual parenting.

Deuteronomy as a Key Biblical Resource on Spiritual Parenting

The entire book of Deuteronomy is framed and presented as the last message of Moses to the children of Israel before his death (1:1–5; 34:1–8). Like a father, indeed a *grand* father of the entire people, Moses is boldly and passionately giving his final remembrances, exhortations, and instructions to the new generation of Israelites after the older generation had perished in the wilderness during the forty years that Israel had been sentenced to sojourn there. This is the crowning moment of Moses's role of spiritual parenting. Just as the fatherhood of Isaac and Jacob comes to culminating expression in Genesis when they respectively bestow final blessings on each of their children, Moses carries out this fatherly responsibility at the end of Deuteronomy by bestowing blessings on each of the twelve tribes of Israel as a final act before his death (33).

Yet Moses does even more than act in the capacity of a father to the children of Israel. He also passes the torch of parenting to the new generation by instructing them on how they are to carry out their own parental responsibilities to the next generation and, by extension, to all subsequent generations in perpetuity. No book in the Bible pays more attention to raising up the next generation and every new generation than the book of Deuteronomy. And no passage in Deuteronomy is more explicitly instructive on this matter than chapter 6. Here we see Moses making a fervent appeal for this new generation of the children of Israel to take up this urgent responsibility of spiritual parenting and to pass it forward from generation to generation.

Could there be a heavier matter, a more gripping burden for a parent? God's parental urgency for faith transmission to every new generation is here reflected in this elder's final words. *God is a passionate Parent* (Deut. 1:31) *speaking through an impassioned parent* (vv. 9–12, cf. 33:1) to his children, who will now bear the weight of carrying forward the family faith unto the generations to come. While this purpose drives the entire book of Deuteronomy, it is brought to a particularly sharp focus in chapter 6. Given the importance of this chapter to the subject of spiritual parenting, we would do well to read each portion of it before considering some comments.

Moses's Teaching in Deuteronomy 6

> Now this is the commandment—the statutes and the ordinances—that the LORD your God charged me to teach you to observe in the land that you are about to cross into and occupy, so that you and your children and your children's children may fear the LORD your God all the days of your life and keep all his decrees and his commandments that I am commanding you, so that your days may be long. Hear therefore, O Israel, and observe them diligently, so that it may go well with you and so that you may multiply greatly in a land flowing with milk and honey, as the LORD, the God of your ancestors, has promised you. (Deut. 6:1–3 NRSV)

Deuteronomy 6 begins by introducing this massive responsibility of generation-to-generation faith transmission with reference to a single command: "Now this is the commandment" (v. 1 NRSV). This phrase announces that what follows is the singular command[21]

---

21. Some translations render the term as a plural ("commandments"), but the Hebrew noun here in Deuteronomy 6:1 is singular. And this singular form of the noun also occurs in the last verse of the chapter, verse 25, thus framing the chapter in a

above all other commandments. It is the command that encompasses all the commandments. This is the one commandment which God's people must keep if the faith is to be kept and if the family is to be kept. And so it is addressed to "you and your children and your children's children . . . all the days of your life . . . so that your days may be long" (v. 2 NRSV). The issue here is not individual longevity. It is not our culture's narrow focus on personal fulfillment and self-realization. It is instead focused on the sustaining of godly family life into the future, having a faith that will carry forward into future generations. God has a long-range goal in view here—a faith connecting the ancestors of the past to the children of the future, "that you may multiply greatly in a land flowing with milk and honey, as the LORD, the God of your ancestors, has promised you" (v. 3 NRSV).

So, what is this single, all-encompassing commandment? It is Israel's golden text.

The Greatest Commandment

"Hear, O Israel: The LORD our God, the LORD is one! You shall love the LORD your God with all your heart, with all your soul, and with all your strength.

"And these words which I command you today shall be in your heart. You shall teach them diligently to your children, and you shall

---

way that encourages seeing the whole chapter as an elaboration of the Shema commandment in verses 4–5.

talk of them [or about them] when you sit in your house, when you walk by the way, when you lie down, and when you rise up. You shall bind them as a sign on your hand, and they shall be as frontlets between your eyes. You shall write them on the doorposts of your house and on your gates." (Deut. 6:4–9)

The Hebrew people came to call the first part of this biblical passage "the Shema," which is Hebrew for the commandment's first word. "Hear [or *Heed, Shema*], O Israel: The LORD our God, the LORD is one! You shall love the LORD your God with all your heart, with all your soul, and with all your strength" (vv. 4–5). Everything begins here. Everything flows from this. It is a call expressed in second-person singular. So it addresses each one of God's people with the command to heed and to love God completely. Jesus Himself identified this as "the greatest commandment" (Matt. 22:36–39; Mark 12:28–30). *The heart of the faith is a faith of the heart*, not merely right actions and right beliefs but a rightness that goes all the way down to our innermost being, our deepest affections, motives, and passions—a heart loving God above all, first and foremost.

The statement following the Shema reinforces this heart focus: "These words . . . shall be in your heart" (v. 6). *Before Godly faith can be in our homes, it must first be in our hearts.* Yet from our hearts, attention is immediately turned to our homes, helping us to see how vitally this family concern is joined to the first concern: "You shall teach them" (that is, these words that are first "in your heart") "to your children" (v. 7). This is the crucial connection and key movement: first *"in your heart,"* then *"to your children."*

We see here that the faith training of our children does not depend upon sophisticated curriculum, special effects, and catchy media. Of all media, God's singular priority and preference is the medium of the human heart. Techniques and methods are rendered miniscule by comparison. Everything depends upon hearts, which are first given over to God and then turned unto the children. As noted in previous chapters, Malachi 4:4–6 ends the entire Old Testament with a climactic acknowledgment related to this point. Either the hearts of elders will be turned to their children and the hearts of children to their elders or there will remain no other prospect for life other than curse.

Teaching the Children

It is no wonder that Scripture elsewhere urges us: "Keep your heart with all diligence, For out of it spring the issues of life" (Prov. 4:23). Here in Deuteronomy 6, out of a heart devoted to God there is expected to come forth a life that generates a new generation, a life that issues in children. It is a vision of children being taught God's life-giving words in every part of every day that makes up our life: "Talk about them when you sit in your house, when you walk by the way, when you lie down, and when you rise up" (v. 7). This is a drawn-out and plain-spoken way of pointing to all the pieces and parts of our daily lives, with no parts excluded, with every part united by the singular word and will of the one God, who alone can make all of our heart and all of our home life to be whole.

After getting the heart right, the directions in Deuteronomy 6 for teaching God's words to the children are remarkably simple, requiring no special training or parenting skills: just "talk about them." Nothing more high-flown than that! Merely and simply, just "talk about them." Nothing is said here about *how* to talk about them or *how much*, but only a concern of *when* to do it. And that would be in every part of the daily round of life. Here again, the instruction is surprisingly simple and mundanely expressed, involving no extraordinary occasions, events, or feats: just "when you sit . . . , when you walk . . . , when you lie down, and when your rise up" (v. 7). Nothing extraordinary is required, no special efforts or times. It is simply to be a matter of ordinary conversations carried out at the most ordinary of times. It is like the point Moses makes later in Deuteronomy, when he says, the word "is not too mysterious for you, nor is it far off. It is not in heaven . . . Nor is it beyond the sea, . . . But the word is very near you, in your mouth and in your heart, that you may do it" (30:11–14).

Such simplicity is a warning against our tendencies to complicate and fragment our lives, to set up a special compartment that we would then identify as our "spiritual life." The point is not to have a special "spiritual life" in this fragmented way, but to have a life that is spiritual and whole through all our daily and ordinary routines and activities.

The Progression of the Impact of God's Word

As one moves through Deuteronomy 6, it is worth noting the progression of impact that God's Word is meant to have in the core aspects of each person's life:

- Your heart (defining your passions):
  "these words . . . shall be in your heart" (6:6)
- Your hand (determining your deeds):
  "bind them . . . on your hand" (6:8a)
- Your head (dominating your thoughts):
  "they shall be . . . on your forehead" (6:8b NASB)

And there is another progression of impact in Deuteronomy 6. It is one that moves from the personal level all the way to the national level, with expanding effects moving outward in space and time:

- From the heart:
  "these words . . . shall be in your heart" (6:6)
- To the home:
  "teach them diligently to your children . . . when you sit . . . walk . . . lie down . . . rise up" (6:7)
  "write them on the doorposts of your house" (6:9a)
- To the city:
  "write them . . . on your gates" (6:9b)
- To the nation:
  "when the LORD your God brings you into the land . . . with great and good cities . . . you shall diligently keep the commandments" (6:10, 17 ESV)

This expansion of impact to the nation as a whole is elaborated in the portion of Deuteronomy 6 that follows:

"And when the Lord your God brings you into the land that he swore to your fathers, to Abraham, to Isaac, and to Jacob, to give you—with great and good cities that you did not build, and houses full of all good things that you did not fill, and cisterns that you did not dig, and vineyards and olive trees that you did not plant—and when you eat and are full, then take care lest you forget the Lord, who brought you out of the land of Egypt, out of the house of slavery. It is the Lord your God you shall fear. Him you shall serve and by his name you shall swear. You shall not go after other gods, the gods of the peoples who are around you—for the Lord your God in your midst is a jealous God—lest the anger of the Lord your God be kindled against you, and he destroy you from off the face of the earth.

"You shall not put the Lord your God to the test, as you tested him at Massah. You shall diligently keep the commandments of the Lord your God, and his testimonies and his statutes, which he has commanded you. And you shall do what is right and good in the sight of the Lord, that it may go well with you, and that you may go in and take possession of the good land that the Lord swore to give to your fathers by thrusting out all your enemies from before you, as the Lord has promised." (vv. 10–19 ESV)

While Deuteronomy 6 lays out this entire sweep (from heart to home to city to nation), the chapter clearly gives special emphasis to the parents' responsibility to teach the children. We see this in the thorough way verses 7–9 spell out this point ("when you sit . . . walk . . . lie down . . . rise up"). And we also see it in the way Moses returns to this matter in the final paragraph of the chapter, to which we now turn our attention.

When Children Question the Rules of Their Parents

"When your son asks you in time to come, 'What is the meaning of the testimonies and the statutes and the rules that the Lord our God has commanded you?' then you shall say to your son, 'We were Pharaoh's slaves in Egypt. And the Lord brought us out of Egypt with a mighty hand. And the Lord showed signs and wonders, great and grievous, against Egypt and against Pharaoh and all his household, before our eyes. And he brought us out from there, that he might bring us in and give us the land that he swore to give to our fathers. And the Lord commanded us to do all these statutes, to fear the Lord our God, for our good always, that he might preserve us alive, as we are this day. And it will be righteousness for us, if we are careful to do all this commandment before the Lord our God, as he has commanded us.'" (Deut. 6:20–25 ESV)

This culminating passage of Deuteronomy 6 offers one of the most important instructions on spiritual parenting in all of Scripture. Notice how it illustrates several of the major points discussed in the previous chapters of this study. First, we see the emphasis on parents teaching their children by means of storytelling (chap. 2). Second, we see focus on a child's question as a key instigating trigger for the teaching moment (chap. 4). Third, we see how this entails the importance of parents listening attentively to their children when the children begin to assert their own independence from their parents (chap. 3).

Building on all these important aspects of parental practice, we also can see in this final paragraph of Deuteronomy 6 a new element of instruction that addresses a particular challenge—one that can be expected as a matter of course in spiritual parenting. It is the challenge that comes when (and note, it's "when," not "if") our children begin raising questions about the God-given rules which they have been taught.

It is important to notice how the children pose the question. They ask about the "rules that the Lord our God has commanded you" (v. 20 ESV). The pronouns used here are quite telling. The children acknowledge "the Lord" as *our* God," but they refer to the "rules" as what God "has commanded *you*." Notice, it is "you" rather than "us." Although the children are still holding to God, they have taken a step toward letting go of God's law. It is a step of disowning or distancing and dissociating themselves from the rules in question.

The Story the Children Need to Hear

This is a moment when parents can be tempted to react, even overreact, to their children's show of resistance.

Perhaps the most common parental reaction is to push back by reaching back no further than the immediate ground of parental authority: "Because I said so." A bit more thoughtful response might be to reach a little further back to the ground of divine authority: "Because God's Word said so." More thoughtful still might be an attempt to defend God's moral directives with ethical reasoning. However, Moses, who is himself speaking on the ground of God's authority (cf. Deut. 1:3), directs parents to follow an alternative course—one that reaches back much further to what I would call "the story of the moral." It is as if the child's question about *"your* rules" should be understood as a signal to the parents that the child is now ready to hear and needing to hear (yes, *Shema*) more than our reactions. They are needing to hear the story of God's actions—the actions of *"our* God" on behalf of *"our* family" that have established the very life and identity and destiny of our family in the first place.

This is the story that not only reaches back but it also reaches forward to include the children in the story. For Moses is surely including them in the pronouns of Deuteronomy 6:21–24, when he says, "*We* were Pharoah's slaves . . . the Lord brought *us* out of Egypt with a mighty hand . . . that he might bring *us* in and give *us* the land that he swore to *our* fathers . . . And the Lord commanded *us* to do all these statutes . . . for *our* good always, that he might preserve *us* alive, as *we* are this day" (ESV, emphasis added).

The children need this story. Their very life depends upon it. For this is the story whereby they can, quite literally, *come to terms* with their identity. It is the story that reveals the identity of God's people as it reveals the identity of God. For it is God's story. He is the subject of the verbs that determine the storyline, as can be noted in the previous passage: "*The* L ORD brought us out . . . that *he* might bring us in and give us the land that *he* swore to our fathers . . . And *the* L ORD commanded us . . . that *he* might preserve us alive, as we are this day" (vv. 21–24 ESV, emphasis added).

God is both the author of this story and the main actor, whose actions and words define and redefine all other characters. Trying to find life and identity outside of this story amounts to living in a false narrative and acting out a false identity. But coming into this story reveals who God knows us to be and then what God calls us to do. For the children, then, what God calls His people to do will make sense to them when and only when they are brought into this story—indeed, "the story of the moral."

Moses is offering God's people here in Deuteronomy 6:20–25 a concise summation of the core story of Old Testament faith—the exodus event. It can stand right alongside the concise summation of the core story of New Testament faith that Jesus offers in John 3:16—the Christ event. In both cases, we are being given the core story that belongs to God's people as a whole. And Moses is explicitly making the point that this core story should be given by parents to their children.

A Closed Creed or an Open-Ended Story

Some scholars have promoted the idea that what we are given in Deuteronomy 6:20–25 is a creedal statement to be memorized and quoted verbatim, such as in a catechism response.[22] As meaningful as this could be, I would suggest that Moses is here calling for much more than this. I would suggest that he is proposing a dynamic, open-ended story[23] that opens up the parent-child conversation, like the one just mentioned a few verses earlier (v. 7).

Just a few verses later in Deuteronomy 7, Moses recites a summation of the storyline of the exodus once again. He does so here in a way that parallels 6:20–25 but also shows that he is not rigidly bound to some precise wording of it:

> "The LORD has brought you out with a mighty hand and redeemed you from the house of slavery, from the hand of Pharaoh king of Egypt. Know therefore that the LORD your God is God, the faithful God who keeps covenant and steadfast love with those who love him and keep his commandments, to a thousand generations." (Deut. 7:8b–9 ESV)

The Israelites were certainly not opposed to summarizing their core story with precise wording intended for memorization, as attested by the way it is set to music

---

22. This theory was initially put forward by Gerhard von Rad, a German Old Testament scholar, who rose to international renown in the mid-twentieth century.

23. I would suggest that Moses's final phrase in Deuteronomy 6:24 (ESV), "as we are this day," even implies Moses's recognition of the open-endedness of the story he is telling, as if to say, this is the story . . . at least "up to this present day."

and verse in quite a few psalms. A good example (in addition to Psalm 78, as previously discussed in chapter 2) is Psalm 136, which presents a poetic recital of Israel's story from the creation of the world (vv. 5–9) to the exodus from Egypt (vv. 10–16) and then on to the conquest of the promised land (vv. 17–24). This psalm might even have been inspired by the words of Moses just quoted from Deuteronomy 7:8–9. Moses sees the deliverance from Egypt in verse 8 as indicative of God's "steadfast love" for his obedient people "to a thousand generations" (v. 9), and Psalm 136 echoes this very idea with the following refrain that occurs twenty-six times throughout this poem: "for his steadfast love endures forever."

This exact same refrain begins Psalm 107. What is remarkable about this psalm is that, instead of presenting a retelling of Israel's national story, there is a series of stanzas that each tells a more particular, exodus-*like* story, belonging to only "some" individuals within Israel. The stanzas are each introduced with parallel phrasing as follows:

- "Some wandered in desert wastes" (v. 4 ESV)
- "Some sat in darkness and in the shadow of death" (v. 10 ESV)
- "Some were fools through their sinful ways" (v. 17 ESV)
- "Some went down to the sea in ships" (v. 23 ESV)

In each case, the stanza's introduction is followed by a brief poetic verse with a storyline that parallels the exodus storyline, even though the circumstances are individualized and different. After a description of the specified situation of distress, the distressed individuals, we are told in each case, "cried to the LORD in their trouble" (vv. 6, 13, 19, 28 ESV), just like in the exodus (cf. Ex. 3:7), and, as in the exodus, the LORD "delivered them from their distress" (cf. Ex. 3:8). Each stanza ends with the refrain, "Let them thank the LORD for his steadfast love, for his wondrous works to the children of man!" (vv. 8, 15, 21, 31 ESV). This call to thankful praise, of course, parallels the exodus storyline's climactic moment when the Israelites sing a song of praise to the Lord right after He has delivered them through the midst of the Red Sea (Ex. 15:1–18; note the reference to God's "steadfast love" in verse 13 ESV). Exodus 15 can be seen as the Bible's first psalm.

Personal Stories Within the Big Story of God's People

Psalm 107, then, directly supports the idea that, within the large story of God's entire people, there are smaller, more personal stories that bear the family resemblance of the larger story and that, likewise, bear being repeated. As the beginning of Psalm 107 itself says, "Let the redeemed of the LORD say so" (v. 2 ESV).[24] This call makes *explicit* what I am suggesting is *implicit* in Moses's instruction to parents in Deuteronomy 6:20–25. And that is this: It is vital to tell our children the big story

---

24. The concluding verse of Psalm 107 reinforces this opening call to "Let the redeemed of the LORD say so" by giving the following exhortation: "Whoever is wise, let him attend to these things; let them consider the steadfast love of the LORD" (v. 43 ESV).

of God's people in terms of its open-ended, continuing storyline—a storyline that is continuing not only in terms of new chapters being added to the big story[25] but also in terms of ongoing and outflowing personal stories of how we ourselves have experienced the truth and parallel reality of the big story in our own individual lives. Yes, our children need to be told the stories of our own personal exodus experiences and of our own wilderness journeys and promised-land moments.

Our questioning children have need of hearing from us this overarching God-story and our own personal God-stories. We need to tell these stories to our children, including our spiritual daughters and sons. We need to tell them these stories, for God's sake. We need to tell them these God-stories as if their lives depended on them, because they do.

A Story of God's Strength and Our Weakness

There is a crucial feature that we should finally not fail to notice in the story that Moses exhorts parents to tell their children in Deuteronomy 6:20–25. This is a story that reveals God's mighty, delivering strength while confessing to our children the unflattering weakness that we bring to the story. "We were Pharaoh's slaves in Egypt" (v. 21 ESV). This is a story that turns on a crucial weak point in the life of God's people rather than on one

---

25. The adding of chapters to the big story, of course, is what allows the narrative of God's people to move all the way forward from the exodus event to the Christ event.

of our power points. "We were slaves." What a humbling, even humiliating, admission!

We are ever tempted to cover up the weaknesses of our past, the humble origins of our history and heritage. These are the kinds of things we want to rise above and leave behind. These are the humbling facts about our lives that usually get scrubbed from our résumés, our social media profiles, and our memories. We practice hiding such things from others, from ourselves, and from our children. And that is how we succeed in training ourselves and our children to be embarrassed and ashamed of parts of ourselves and themselves. And that is how we fail to realize that it is costing us and them key and core parts of their identities and ours, of knowing who we really are. Yet the Word of God and, by implication, the God of the Word, shows no embarrassment about these weak points.

Throughout the book of Deuteronomy, Moses practices what he preaches in this matter of confessing weaknesses. In the stories he recounts to the children of Israel, Moses bears witness not only to the humble origins he shares with his people but also to his own personal weaknesses in humbling moments of inability and inadequacy (Deut. 1:9–12; 9:17–19; 31:1–2). At multiple points he even recalls his most humiliating moment of moral failure—failure that brought God's judgment of preventing him from entering the promised land (1:37; 3:26–27; 32:48–52).

We can see this same kind of pattern again and again throughout Scripture as one of the major characteristics of so many of the stories of major characters of the Bible.

Consider the accounts of the weaknesses and failings of Abraham, Jacob, Samson, David, Peter, or Saul before he became Paul. In the next chapter, we will consider how this pattern is presented in a particularly pronounced and exemplary way in the story of Elijah, who also, like Moses, becomes a biblical model of spiritual parenting.

Perhaps Moses deserves no small amount of the credit for helping to establish this pattern of self-humbling testimony. For throughout Deuteronomy, we see him teaching and modeling the kind of storytelling to the next generation that honors God by being honest about ourselves. We might be tempted to think, *If I acknowledge such personal weaknesses to my children, they will lose respect for me.* However, God's Word calls for God's people to prioritize protecting *His* honor instead of our own (5:6–11) and to leave the matter of our children's honoring of us in the hands of God (v. 16).

One of the ways that our children's honor for us will then manifest is when they find our honest-to-God stories worth remembering, even to the point of claiming these stories as their own. Then our stories and their stories will be drawn together into a story we both can own and share together—God's own story. This will be *our testimony*—what I like to define as *the story we tell when God gets us told!*

CHAPTER 5

OUR WEAK POINTS TURNED INTO STRONG LINKS

[Elijah] went a day's journey into the wilderness and came and sat down under a broom tree. And he asked that he might die, saying, "It is enough; now, O Lord, take away my life, for I am no better than my fathers."

—1 Kings 19:4 ESV

Elijah could well be considered the patron saint of spiritual parenting in the Bible. As discussed previously in chapter 1, this prophet of the Old Testament is called upon to play an eldering role in the New Testament. Along with Moses on the Mount of Transfiguration, Elijah makes a posthumous appearance as an elder to Jesus, no less! It is no wonder that Elijah is chosen for this role, given all the emphasis that his story in First and Second Kings places on his spiritual parenting.

However, the quotation of Elijah in 1 Kings 19:4, which comes in the middle of his story, reflects a point at which Elijah sees nothing in his life that could ever lead him to expect such a glorious end. Nothing that would lead him to anticipate his legacy of being a heart-turning restorer of spiritual parenting to future generations, as Malachi 4:5–6 indicates. Yet then again, Elijah's role as a paragon of spiritual parenting is perhaps even more significant and relevant to us precisely *because* his noteworthy weaknesses do not prevent him from becoming such an exemplary figure.

This chapter will focus upon what the story of Elijah can show us and teach us about spiritual parenting, in the light of Elijah's role model for this in Scripture. Particular attention will be given to the weak points in Elijah's life, for they figure prominently, as we shall see, in how God raises him up in his parental calling. By God's gracious interventions, Elijah's weak points, you could say, are turned into strong links with his spiritual children, and not just for the sake of his own generation but also for the spiritual parenting of all generations to come. To help set the stage for this discussion, the following brief review of Elijah's story should be helpful.

The Story of Elijah

Elijah was a prophet who lived and prophesied in northern Israel during the ninth century BC when the Hebrew tribes were divided into two kingdoms, North and South. He confronted the challenge of Ahab, King of Israel, and his foreign wife, Jezebel from Tyre, who vigorously attempted to establish Baal worship in northern Israel during this time. Elijah's story can be viewed in terms of five main acts.

In the first act (1 Kings 17), Elijah appears from out of nowhere to declare God's judgment on the nation in the form of a drought. God then immediately commands Elijah to go into hiding. First, he goes and camps beside a small brook where God sustains him by sending ravens with food scraps. Soon the brook dries up, and God then tells Elijah to travel to the foreign town of Zarephath near Tyre, where he would find a certain widow who would provide for him there. He arrives to find that the widow is down to her last meal for herself and her little boy. All three end up surviving through the duration of the drought by a miraculous provision of oil and meal that keep showing up in the widow's containers, according to Elijah's prophetic promise.

A second crisis in the widow's house comes when her son becomes ill and dies, prompting the mother to confront Elijah and his God as being somehow responsible. Elijah then takes the lifeless son from his mother and carries him to his guest room, where he repeatedly drapes himself upon the child's body and cries out to God. In response, God brings the child back to life, thereby convincing the woman of Elijah's prophetic status and authority.

In the second act (1 Kings 18), God commands Elijah to go show himself to King Ahab, who has sent out a search party to have the prophet arrested. When king and prophet meet, Elijah, whom the king calls the "troubler of Israel" (v. 17), directs the king to convene a gathering of all the prophets of Baal for a contest with Elijah atop Mount Carmel in order to determine who represents the true God. Elijah wins the contest when God sends fire from heaven to consume the sacrifice offered by his true prophet. Elijah then executes the false prophets of Baal before interceding for the return of rain, which soon comes and brings the three-year drought to an end.

In the third act (1 Kings 19), Queen Jezebel, after being told the results of the contest on Carmel, puts a hit out on Elijah, who then flees for his life into the wilderness. After a day's journey, he stops to rest under a broom tree and asks God to take his life. Instead, God feeds him and then directs him to journey further into the wilderness until he reaches Horeb (a.k.a. Sinai), the mountain of God. Here God once again encounters Elijah, but chooses to show up not in a wind, nor in an earthquake, nor in a fire, but instead in "a still small voice" (v. 12)—a voice that directs Elijah to descend the mountain and to go anoint a new generation of leaders, including Elisha as a "prophet in your place" (v. 16).

In the following scene, Elijah finds Elisha plowing in a field, and he throws his mantle upon Elisha and keeps on walking. Elisha responds by running after Elijah and requesting his permission to go back and bid farewell to his parents—a request that elicits Elijah's questioning response, "Go back again, for what have I done to you?" (v. 20). Elisha then goes back and offers his farm animals and equipment as a sacrifice and then returns to follow Elijah and become his servant.

In the fourth act (1 Kings 21), Elijah is called by God to bring a word of judgment against Ahab and Jezebel after they carry out a conspiracy to steal a coveted vineyard near the palace of the royal couple. They have the innocent owner of the vineyard, Naboth, arrested and executed on false charges. Elijah delivers the divine word of judgment to King Ahab when he goes to take possession of the vineyard, declaring to the king that, as with Naboth's blood, dogs would lick the blood of the royal couple and God would bring their royal house to an end (vv. 19–24).

When Ahab dies, there is a following scene (2 Kings 1) in which Ahab's son, Ahaziah, becomes injured in a fall and sends messengers to seek an answer from Baal as to whether he would survive or die. Elijah intercepts these messengers and sends them back to Ahaziah with a rebuke for seeking Baal instead of the God of Israel. Ahaziah then sends a series of military units back to Elijah to capture him, but after the prophet calls down fire from heaven that annihilates two batches of soldiers, Elijah accompanies a surrendering third group back to the king and delivers a word directly to him that he would soon die, and he does.

The fifth and final act (2 Kings 2) begins with the acknowledgment that God was about to bring Elijah's life on earth to an end. This comes as unsettling news to the so-called "sons of the prophets," who are now close followers of Elijah, but it is especially unsettling for Elisha who is clearly the leading member of this group. Elijah tells Elisha not to follow him any further as he leaves to go toward the place of his departure, but Elisha replies with a solemn oath that he will not leave Elijah's side. They go to another place where this same interaction takes place between the two of them, and then to a third place where this same exchange is repeated. Then they come to the Jordan where the river splits, in Red Sea fashion, as Elijah strikes the water with his mantle. When they cross to the other side, Elijah asks Elisha what parting gift he could give to his young follower. Elisha makes the demanding request for "a double portion" of Elijah's spirit (v. 9). Elijah replies that his request will be granted on the condition that Elisha remains with him to the end. Then a heavenly spectacle appears, featuring horses and chariots of fire accompanied by a whirlwind that takes Elijah up into heaven, leaving his mantle to fall down to the earth. Elisha exclaims, "My father, my father! The chariots of Israel and its horsemen!" (v. 12 ESV). Then he picks up the fallen mantle, carries it to the Jordan River, and strikes the water, saying, "Where is the LORD, the God of Elijah?" (v. 14). The river then divides once again, to mark the transition from Elijah to Elisha.

Elijah as a Father Figure

It is important to see that Elijah was raised up by God during a time when Baal worship was being raised up as an alternative faith in Israel. Baal worship was fertility worship. Baal was being sought and served as the source of fertility, whether in flock, in field, or in family. Through Elijah, God was declaring and demonstrating to Israel that He, not Baal, was the true source of fertility. As Elijah lifted up the true fertility power and the fatherhood of the God of Israel, God raised up Elijah as a true father of Israel. Elijah's fatherly identity can be seen in his story at numerous points.

We see this in the dramatic way Elijah's mantle is passed to his successor, Elisha (1 Kings 19:19; 2 Kings 2:13). In connection with this, Elijah becomes a prime biblical exemplar of bestowing a parental blessing when he leaves a "double portion" of his spirit to Elisha at his wondrous departure from his earthly life (2 Kings 2:9–10). This represents a spiritualized expression of the ancient Hebrew law, found in Deuteronomy 21:17, which directed a "double portion" of the parent's inheritance to be given to the oldest son. As Elijah is caught up to heaven, his fathering role to Elisha and all the other "sons of the prophets" (2 Kings 2:3, 5, 7) is explicitly highlighted in Elisha's exclamatory words, "My father, my father! The chariots of Israel and its horsemen!" (v. 12).

Yet most significant of all is the way Scripture identifies Elijah's legacy both at the end of the Old Testament and at the beginning of Luke's Gospel in the New Testament. Elijah is finally known for his inspired role in turning the hearts of fathers to sons and of sons to fathers before the day of the LORD (Mal. 4:5–6; Luke 1:16–17). Elijah's life comes to a climactic end in the blessing of a spiritual son, and then he becomes the enduring figure in Scripture of God's end-time promise to reunite the hearts of parents and their children.

Elijah as an *Unlikely* Father Figure

It is remarkable that Elijah's legacy arrives at this end in view of how the biblical story of Elijah begins. He is introduced in 1 Kings 17:1 only as "Elijah the Tishbite" without reference to any father. We are told *where* Elijah comes from (Tishbe) but not *who* he comes from. This breaks the biblical and ancient cultural convention of identifying a person by referencing the father of that individual ("X, the son of Y"). It is like hearing Elijah's given name but not his last name. One can scarcely find another Old Testament character of such magnitude whose father and all other ancestral identifiers are completely lacking.[26] Is this a silence that says something? I would suggest that it is telling us about a fathering deficit in Elijah's life that reflects a fathering deficit in Israel—one that Elijah is being raised up to address. There is support for this in the words we later see Elijah praying under the broom tree at the low point of his story: "It is enough! Now, LORD, take my life, for I am no better than my fathers" (1 Kings 19:4). Elijah is clearly indicating a fathering deficiency that reaches all the way down to the personal level for him. Yet this "fatherless" one is the very one whose story will end with Elisha's reverent words of veneration: "My father, my father! The chariots of Israel and its horsemen!" (2 Kings 2:12).

---

26. One could perhaps cite Daniel as a comparable example. His lack of genealogical identification in the book of Daniel might serve to register the force of the break in family connections and native identity that the Babylonian captors were deliberately aiming to carry out, as the story of Daniel 1 seems intent to show (see esp. verse 7).

Steps in Elijah's Journey to Fatherhood

How does Elijah get from his fatherless introduction (1 Kings 17:1) to this fatherly conclusion? The story of the widow of Zarephath and her son in 1 Kings 17:8–24, I would suggest, conveys an important step in this significant transformational journey. This story contains two episodes. The first (vv. 8–16) involves the Lord's provision in the area of agricultural fertility, through the miraculous supply of meal and oil. But the second is focused on the Lord's power of fertility in raising up human offspring (vv. 17–24).

Elijah is introduced to the widow's son in the first episode (v. 12). This son, like Elijah, is fatherless and now dependent on this widow woman for his life. But in the second episode, the identification between Elijah and this son goes to another level. The son falls sick and dies, his mother confronts the "man of God" with this tragedy, and Elijah says, "Give me your son" (v. 18–19a). And with words that seem to accentuate the transfer of the son's close connection from the mother to the prophet, we read, "So he took him out of her arms and carried him to the upper room where he was staying, and laid him on his own bed" (v. 19b).

Still the identification between this man and this child goes one dramatic step further. In this upper room, we see a pivotal moment in Elijah's character development. For the first time in the Elijah story, we no longer see Elijah in the role of the mighty prophet wielding supernatural power. In a scene of desperation that virtually matches that of the mother, Elijah cries to the Lord.

"Then he cried out to the LORD, 'LORD my God, have you brought tragedy even on this widow I am staying with, by causing her son to die?' Then he stretched himself out on the boy three times and cried out to the LORD, 'LORD my God, let this boy's life return to him!'" (vv. 20–21 NIV). That's right, we are made privy to a scene of a grown man crying. Next, we are told that the Lord heard Elijah's voice, the child's breath came into him again, and Elijah brought him down and gave him to his mother, saying, "See, your son lives!" (vv. 22–23). If ever there was a scene that could represent the experience of becoming a spiritual parent, this surely is it!

So we see that, on his way to becoming God's prime model and mediator of reuniting and raising up future generations, Elijah first raises up the son of a single mother in Zarephath before raising up Elisha and the other sons of the prophets.

Elijah's Weak Points Turned into Strong Links

What stands out in Elijah's unfolding path to spiritual parenting is how his most pivotal steps turn not on his strong points but rather on his weak points. One could even say that, in the matter of Elijah's spiritual parenting, God's strength was made perfect in Elijah's weaknesses (cf. 2 Cor. 12:9).

Elijah raises up the widow's son only after the key turning point of coming to the desperation of crying out to God while draping himself three times on the body of the dead child. It's almost as if Elijah's weakness merges with that of the lifeless boy at this point. And

Elijah raises up Elisha as his successor only after the key turning point of coming to the desperation of praying that God would take his own life, which he sees as "no better than my fathers" (1 Kings 19:4). At this very point, God gives Elijah enough strength to journey on to the mountain of God, where he receives God's call to anoint successors of the next generation (vv. 9–18).

Yet the narrative's depiction of Elijah's weaknesses does not stop there. When Elijah proceeds to carry out his call to anoint the next generation, he still appears at multiple points to be at a loss as to what to do. After coming down from the mountain of God, he meets Elisha plowing in a field, throws his mantle on Elisha, and then moves on, so that Elisha must run to catch up to him. Elisha then requests Elijah's permission to return and kiss his parents goodbye before following Elijah, prompting Elijah to say to him, "Go back again, for what have I done to you?" (vv. 19–20). In this moment, Elijah appears far less certain than Elisha in knowing what to do. Elisha responds to Elijah's indecisive question with decisive actions. He goes back, slaughters his oxen, cooks the meat by burning the wooden ox yokes, effectively burning his bridge behind him, and feeds his people. "Then," we are told, "he arose and followed Elijah, and became his servant" (v. 21).

When we come to the Elijah narrative's final episode, which recounts his departure (2 Kings 2:1–18), Elijah once again appears to be a step behind his successor, Elisha, in knowing what to do. It is Elisha rather than Elijah who acts with foresight and takes the initiative in the steps leading up to the bestowal of the parental blessing. Elisha, who is aware that his mentor will soon depart (v. 3), insists on sticking close to Elijah as the old prophet journeys toward his exit point. At three separate junctures along the way, Elijah tells Elisha to stay behind and not follow him any further. However, Elisha resolutely refuses each time with a solemn oath to stick with his mentor (vv. 2, 4, 6). This leads up to the older prophet finally inviting the younger to propose some parting gift, which prompts Elisha's bold request for a double portion of spirit (v. 9). As if taken aback by such a request, Elijah says, "You have asked a difficult thing" (v. 10 NIV). This response is quite remarkable in the way it reveals, once again, Elijah's sense of being out of his depth as he comes to this most climactic moment of spiritual parenting. Yet after acknowledging the difficulty, he proceeds to say to Elisha, "Nevertheless, if you see me when I am taken from you, it shall be" (v. 10). Ironically, Elisha's previously demonstrated insistence on sticking with Elijah now becomes the very precondition for obtaining his spiritual father's blessing and mantle. And even this transaction comes not by way of its being enacted by Elijah but rather by Elijah's being acted upon, indeed being "taken" (vv. 9, 11).

So from start to finish, Elijah's success as a spiritual parent comes not from his *knowing* what to do but rather despite his *not knowing* what to do. In the end he becomes Scripture's prime model of spiritual parenting by repeatedly coming to the end of himself. And we are shown how this happens to him in the upper room in Zarephath, under the broom tree in the wilderness, in the field where he first meets Elisha, and on the other side of the Jordan River right before he is taken up. It would appear, then, that Scripture has uplifted Elijah as a model of spiritual parenting in a way that uplifts a humbling truth. Our successful fulfillment of this intergenerational responsibility will no doubt turn on the Elijah pattern of facing our weaknesses rather than looking to our strengths, even leaning into our not knowing rather than depending on our know-how.

Summary

- Elijah was raised up to be a key model and catalyst of spiritual parenting.
- He didn't come to this calling by having a good role model himself, because he didn't.
- The success of Elijah's spiritual parenting turned on his weak points, not his strong points.
- These weak points become the turning points of the stories that link the generations together.
- God showing up at our weakest points is the key link that brings disconnected generations into one another's stories—yes, all of us together into the same story.
- This is the kind of story that holds God's promise to transform and to turn our hearts.

A Personal Story of How God Can Turn Weak Points into Strong Links

Here is how these humbling truths about spiritual parenting began to take root in me. When Jean and I were raising our daughters in their preschool years, Hannah's diagnosis of cerebral palsy brought with it a multitude of medical interventions and doctors' appointments that kept us very busy. What's more, Hannah required enormous amounts of daily care and attention from Jean and me that otherwise would have been shared more evenly with Hannah's older sister. It's often the case that a younger sibling will steal the spotlight from an older sibling, but in Hannah's case this was much more pronounced. I could see Emily reacting to this at times by acting up with disruptive behaviors—nothing, to be sure, out of the normal range of stuff arising from sibling rivalry. As this situation dragged on, it dragged me down with a mixture of feelings. I frequently felt frazzled and frustrated at Emily's behaviors. At the same time, I often felt sorry for her over what I suspected was hiding underneath. Most of all, I felt like I was failing as a father, but I was mostly hiding this feeling, even from myself. I was totally at a loss in knowing what to do to help either of my daughters with their respective challenges, one highly visible and the other deeply hidden.

One day in a vulnerable moment just outside my seminary office door, I was met by one of my seminary students, who happened to be a missionary on furlough from the Philippines, old enough to be my mother. When she asked me how I was doing, I cracked the door and sheepishly let her in on the burden I was carrying for my two daughters. I could take you to the spot where I was standing when she looked at me with a piercing gaze and spoke with what I would now describe as a holy maternal authority. She said, "You need to realize something today. Of all the men in the world, you are the one God has chosen to be the father of your two daughters. It's not about knowing what to do. It's about knowing who you are." As God as my witness, that one word spoken to me that day by this woman named Marcia Anderson has come to mean more to me than all the academic diplomas and awards that hang on my wall. That word placed a touchstone of solid rock beneath my feet, and by God's grace I have gone back to it again and again whenever my steps as a spiritual father have strayed, stumbled, or become unsteady.

One such time came just a year or two later. The burden of Hannah's cerebral palsy did not become lighter. It pressed down more heavily on me personally to the point of exposing some major weak points in my life. The most consequential of these appeared when Jean, as a stay-at-home mom, began to develop back problems as Hannah became heavier and the risks of heavy lifting became well-nigh impossible to avoid. I tried very hard to help when I could, but I was not at home during the day. As Jean began to struggle with her back pain, I began to struggle with a much more hidden pain that, up to that point, I had been suppressing. When Hannah's diagnosis of cerebral palsy was first shared with us at her one-year checkup, Jean let herself enter the grief of it all. I didn't. Without realizing it, I kicked that can down the road. But now that Hannah was four and Jean's back was hurting, I was finally catching up to that can. It had become too big to kick, and I was not at all ready to open it.

But I read somewhere that God can open things that no man can keep shut. Oh my, but did this truth ever come home to me! At that very time, my father had an open-heart surgery. When he was still in the hospital but well on his way to recovery, Jean and I, together with Emily and Hannah, went to visit my father in his hospital room. My mother was there, along with my older brother and his wife. It was a happy visit, and I was not eager to bring it to a conclusion. But Jean, in view of the long drive home and nighttime chores ahead of us, started gently nudging me toward bringing our visit to an end. She finally said to me in her very gentle way, "Honey, why don't you help me?" Jean was wanting my help getting both girls and Hannah's special equipment loaded into our van.

At that moment, my brother, who is a very wise and loving brother to me, flashed his eyes at me and said with what seemed like an edge in his voice, "Yes, why don't you help her?" It did not feel like an appeal for momentary help but instead like a very intentional accusation against how I had been living my life. If he only knew how much I had been trying to help! Trying to help day after day . . . trying to do all I could to ease the ever-increasing load that was pressing down on Jean's weak spine. All the while feeling helpless, unable to do a blessed thing to stop the mounting damage, like watching a train wreck in slow-motion. But as soon as these defensive thoughts flared up in me, Jean echoed my brother's words with, "Yes, why don't you help me?" Her tone was playful and did not carry the undertone of accusation that I was sensing behind my brother's words. Yet what mattered to me in that moment was that Jean, of all people, knew how I was helping; my brother didn't know, and Jean suddenly had become a witness for the prosecution instead of a witness for my defense.

Rage! That's what I suddenly felt. I didn't say a word, at least not until Jean and I and the girls were all loaded up in the van. As I floored the gas pedal and squealed the tires leaving the hospital parking lot, I exploded on Jean and unloaded both barrels of my case against her failure to stand up for me. She was defenseless before the barrage of my accusation. She apologized profusely and began to weep. I was so angry that even this did not help walk me back from my rage. I sped down the interstate, seething in silence as Jean sobbed. And finally, it began to sink in. I had a problem. Yes, I had a problem, and it wasn't in Jean. It was in me. The exchange in the hospital room was way too small to account for a rage that enormous. Why was I so angry? Where was all this combustion coming from? What was underneath it? Why was I so triggered when my help for Jean was questioned? It finally occurred to me, somewhere in the silence of our ride home that night, that I simply did not know the answers to these questions.

Over the next few days, I got tired of asking these questions to myself, and I somehow found the grace to ask God. I did not receive any answer from God quickly. I suspect the delay might have been a divine test to see how serious I was in asking the questions. Then early one morning, I got quiet enough in my quiet time to hear a "still small voice" say this to me: "You're helping Jean carry the physical burden of Hannah but not the spiritual burden." What a slap in the face! I thought, *I pray all the time! What more could I do than I'm already doing to carry the spiritual burden of Hannah?* As this question dangled unanswered within me over the next few days, it also turned into a prayer, a rather testy prayer, as if to dare God to show me, "What more could I do?!"

Then one night as I was about to climb into bed, I was suddenly struck by a thought that came with crystal clarity out of the blue. And I knew instantly that it had come as an answer to my question, "What more could I do?" It took the form of these words: "Why don't you carry Hannah forward to the altar of your church for prayer?" I immediately thought, *What if I did this and nothing happened?* In a split second after I had this thought, it was as if God had overheard my thought and was ready with the immediate reply, "If nothing happened, then you would look as weak as Hannah." Busted! I didn't need anyone to tell me that I had just been thrust through by the convicting Word of God, which the writer of Hebrews describes as "sharper than any two-edged sword, piercing to the division of soul and spirit, of joints and of marrow, and discerning the thoughts and intentions of the heart" (4:12 ESV).

The next morning was Palm Sunday, and I got ready for church. But a triumphal entry was the last thing on my mind. When our pastor came to the pulpit that morning, he began by announcing that he did not have a Palm Sunday message. Instead, he had felt compelled to bring a message on the biblical story of King Hezekiah in 2 Kings 19, where the army of the Assyrian Empire came and besieged Jerusalem, demanding an unconditional surrender. But instead of surrendering, Hezekiah turned to God, who answered the king's prayer by mysteriously decimating the Assyrian army during the night and delivering the city.

The pastor's message on that Palm Sunday morning focused on the moment when Hezekiah went to the temple and spread before the Lord a letter of ultimatum from the King of Assyria. My heart was pounding as my pastor approached the climax of his message, and I heard him say these words: "I believe someone needs to get bold enough to spread their problem before the Lord." When he said these words, I could not wait another second. I stood up, reached out, and lifted Hannah from her mother's arms. I then looked down and saw Hannah's crutches lying in the vacant pew in front of me. I reached and grabbed them and then walked to the altar with Hannah in my arms. I stopped near the end of the center aisle in front of the pulpit, throwing the crutches on the floor. I can still remember the sound of those crutches when they bounced on the carpet.

So what happened? Nothing . . . and everything. Nothing in the way of what I was hoping to see. Everything in the way of what God was wanting me to see. Nothing as far as Hannah's continuing need for those crutches. Everything as far as my continuing need to confess my neediness. Nothing in terms of a transformation of Hannah's body. Everything in terms of a turning of my heart.

I would add that when the pastor called for the elders of the church to come forward and pray with us on that Palm Sunday morning in 1989, many people came forward, some to pray and many others to spread their needs before the Lord. And to this day I meet people who tell me that they often remember that day. I often remember it too. I remember it as a day when Jesus made a triumphal entry into our lives and into the heart of my relationship with my daughter Hannah.

A Message by My Daughter

More than two decades down the road from that eventful Palm Sunday morning, my daughter Hannah composed and delivered the following homily before the New Covenant Church of God congregation in Cleveland, Tennessee. In this homily she offers reflections on Paul's comments in Romans 4 on Abraham's struggle to sustain faith in God's promise. And she does this by giving self-revealing testimony of her own moments of profound weakness. She tells of her Elijah-like struggle with depression, the test it has posed to her own faith in the promises of God, and how she, too, has found sustaining strength in the "still small voice."

"Homily" by Hannah Elizabeth Moore

The apostle Paul in his letter to the Romans presents the following powerful statement about hope and faith in the promises of God:

Against all hope, Abraham in hope believed and so became the father of many nations, just as it had been said to him, "So shall your offspring be." Without weakening in his faith, he faced the fact that his body was as good as dead—since he was about a hundred years old—and that Sarah's womb was also dead. Yet he did not waver through unbelief regarding the promise of God, but he was strengthened in his faith and gave glory to God, being fully persuaded that God had power to do what he had promised. (Rom. 4:18–21 NIV)

I think a lot these days about the promises of God. Maybe many of us do. All through the process of writing this reflection, I have wondered, *How honest do I want to be, as I revisit my own experience with God's promises?* And as tempting as it is to make everything sound lovely and nice, I have decided that I cannot in good conscience address the topic at hand without being real. So, at the risk that this will probably end up sounding more like a testimony than a homily, here goes.

My closest friends and family already know this truth about me, and they have been faithful to walk through it with me, but the painful truth is this: For a while now, I've been in full-on combat with depression. Some of the worst I've ever experienced, in fact. Over the past year and a half or so, as the darkness has kept getting darker, I've spent a lot of energy trying to figure out why I am struggling so with depression. Even though I should know better, my brain keeps insisting, *Maybe if I understood it, I could fix it, and I would get well.*

On the surface, it might seem to be easy to identify why I'm depressed. There is this relentless pain and affliction in my physical body that is simply taking its toll on my heart and mind. But I believe there's something else. Something deeper.

Probably like many of you who are taking in my words right now, I am waiting on the fulfillment of a promise from God. Yes, I try very hard not to insist that the fulfillment must look a certain way. And I do not pretend to understand the specifics of what God might have in mind for me. But I do know this much: The promise I carry goes far beyond anything I would ever dare to ask for.

To be truthful, I think much of my depression can be attributed to the sheer mismatch between the wholeness I believe God has promised me—in whatever form that might take—versus the profound brokenness that my daily life entails . . . every single minute of every single day. More times than I can count, I have asked God, "Do You want me to let go of the promise?" *After all,* so my thinking goes, *perhaps it wasn't even from Him!* Maybe the true source was my vain imaginations . . . and those of the well-intentioned people who love me so dearly. Anyone—especially the person I know myself to be—could have misinterpreted.

And even if the promise is true, I've followed Christ long enough to know this piercing truth: Sometimes God requires us to place that which we treasure most on the altar before Him. And so again, I pose a question: Does He wish for me to place this promise on the altar? To this second question, I believe the answer is yes. Yes, He does, because He wants me to die to my own ideas of what fulfillment of the promise should look like. In time, God might even call me to return to the altar and take up the promise once more. So, I must hold the promise very gently and gingerly, without grabbing or grasping.

Yet back to the first question: Does God want me to let go of the promise altogether? This is how I find myself thinking about a response to this question: I often meditate on what the term *faith* means. Sure, Hebrews 11:1 tells us, "Faith is the substance of things hoped for, the evidence of things not seen." But what does that actually look like? For a long time, like many Christians I know, I tended to see faith as some mysterious, powerful force. And if I could muster up enough of it, something miraculous would happen. But slowly, I am learning that there is more—*so* much more to faith than this.

For one thing, faith isn't a force to be mustered up so that something big will happen. On the contrary, I'm beginning to see that faith is that which somehow has us holding onto God and what He has promised, even when—*especially* when—*nothing* big happens . . . when you're left just trying to make it the best you can, wading through the pain and the tears and the nitty-gritty of daily living.

Some in our predominantly and pervasively earthbound culture might think it's all too easy to see one's own wild dream as being grounded in a promise of God. The harder thing, they say, is to knuckle down and do the real work of accepting things as they are. But I see it differently. For me, it is actually much harder to hold onto the promise. Because everything—my entire present reality—shouts the contrary.

Just a few weeks ago, I received yet another troubling medical diagnosis. And I won't try to use pretty words. It was like getting smashed in the gut by a heavyweight boxer. So once again, I asked the Lord: "Shall I let go of the promise? Perhaps I've discerned it all wrong up until now. Maybe this is Your final signal that I really should just give it up." But then a still, small voice in my heart said differently.

I would have let go of the promise, but the promise—and the God who made it—would not let go of *me*. So, there's no letting go, even when everything around me screams that the promise cannot possibly be true. And believe me, sometimes it screams louder than you can imagine. So perhaps that's a bit like what the apostle Paul had in mind in the Scripture text quoted, when he wrote about Abraham "hoping against hope."

Can you imagine how Abraham and Sarah must have felt after God made such an impossible promise? And after time kept passing? Year after year after year? Their bodies got older. Frailer. Yet still, the hoped-for child did not come. And they might have come very near to forsaking the promise. I'm not sure, but I would venture a guess that Abraham laid this promise on the altar many times. Even before his son was born, God may have been preparing Abraham for when he would *literally* lay the very fulfillment of that promise—Isaac himself—on the altar.

So Scripture tells us, Abraham didn't give up. Not even when he got so old that he knew his body was as good as dead. Indeed, Abraham did not let go of the promise. He may have faltered along the way, but he didn't let go. And neither did God. After all, who else but God could underwrite the statement that Abraham "was strengthened in his faith"? And I somehow find strength in this for myself to keep on saying, "Perhaps I should also not let go." I can let every breath I take be a statement of faith. I choose to live. And for me, that choice cannot be separated from choosing to believe—to believe that God will do and is doing what He has promised.

In closing, I will say this: At times I have worried that my holding onto the promise for the future hinders me from serving God in the present. But I'm coming more and more to believe that holding onto God's promise for the future is an important part of serving God in the present. It is bearing witness, for God's sake, as one who walks daily in the tension between the "already" and the "not yet." For me, this is faith.

CHAPTER 6

THE SPIRIT OF SPIRITUAL PARENTING

Mary said to the angel, "How will this be, since I am a virgin?"

And the angel answered her, "The Holy Spirit will come upon you, and the power of the Most High will overshadow you; therefore the child to be born will be called holy—the Son of God. And behold, your relative Elizabeth in her old age has also conceived a son, and this is the sixth month with her who was called barren. For nothing will be impossible with God." And Mary said, "Behold, I am the servant of the Lord; let it be to me according to your word."

—Luke 1:34–38a ESV

Being a Witness to a Spiritual Outpouring

As many readers of this book will know, in February 2023, a spiritual outpouring of immense proportions took place on the campus of Asbury University in Wilmore, Kentucky, in what is now widely known as the Asbury Outpouring. This sixteen-day visitation of the Holy Spirit was directly experienced by on-site witnesses that numbered into the thousands, even tens of thousands, to include many who came from distant parts of the world. This event was conveyed to millions more across the globe through social media as well as conventional news outlets.[27]

I was not a firsthand witness to this happening at Asbury. But a small group of Lee University students, whom I know quite well, went to Asbury on that very first weekend after the outpouring began. This student group, which included leaders of a campus prayer ministry called Lee Prayer, with whom I serve as senior advisor, piled into a couple of vehicles and made the four-hour drive from our campus in Cleveland, Tennessee, to the Asbury campus.

After the weekend, these students returned in time to attend their Monday-morning classes at Lee. In one of these classes—namely, a course on postmodern philosophy—some of these students began sharing testimonies of what they had seen, heard, and experienced at Asbury. This led to one of the students asking the professor whether he would be open to going with them to the Lee Chapel so they could join in a prayer together

---

27. For an excellent, well-researched account of the Asbury Outpouring, which is replete with many statistics and details of its reach and magnitude, see Mark Elliott, *Taken by Surprise: The Asbury Revival of 2023* (Seedbed Publishing, 2023).

for a similar visitation of God's Spirit on the Lee campus. The professor readily agreed, and he and about a dozen students left the class, went directly to the chapel, and began to pray and worship in a simple, spontaneous way.

Before long these few began to sense a Holy Presence, and they began texting their friends with the news that "something is happening in the Lee Chapel!" Several of these text messages reached me. By early afternoon I arrived to witness the chapel sanctuary filling with dozens more, gaining the attention of university administrators, who began to realize the need to make security and schedule decisions to accommodate the possibility that this gathering might grow and continue through the night and even beyond. It did. For the next eight days and nights this meeting continued nonstop, and Lee University experienced, in many similar ways, what was being experienced simultaneously, albeit on a much larger scale, at Asbury University.

Because of my role in Lee Prayer, the university administration approached and authorized me near the outset to be the person designated to stay with the students through that first night and then during subsequent shifts, alongside other Lee personnel, across the remainder of those eight days. Before the week was over, hundreds of Lee students and hundreds of visitors near and far came to the chapel sanctuary to experience this outpouring. It was clear to so many of us who entered fully into that sanctuary of Abiding Presence that we were witnessing something we would long remember and cherish and that, going forward, we would be witnesses to the wonder of it all.

To stand beneath the downflow of such an outpouring is enough to leave anyone with a sense of having too much to tell. Yet there is one moment I experienced on that first night that I have found to be especially worth telling. At one point I stood and addressed the students who were surrounding me in the altar area in front of the sanctuary stage, some standing, some sitting, some kneeling. For me it was a moment of addressing the same question that was posed at the original outpouring of God's Spirit on the day of Pentecost in Acts 2: "What does this mean?" (v. 12 RSV). I recalled to the students how Peter stood up on that day and declared: "This is what was spoken by the prophet Joel: 'And in the last days it shall be, God declares, that I will pour out my Spirit on all flesh, and your sons and your daughters shall prophesy, and your young men shall see visions, and your old men shall dream dreams'" (vv. 16–17 RSV).

It is one thing to quote this text on an average day, but it is altogether another thing to speak this Scripture while standing in the very midst of what appears to be an actual fulfillment of it in real time. As soon as I spoke these words, a student named Micah on the stage behind me shouted, "Dr. Moore, I have a question. Can your dream be my vision?" His words struck me like a lightning bolt of revelation. In all my years of reading this verse of Scripture and quoting it and teaching it and acknowledging the intergenerational component of it, I had never seen what occurred to me in that instant. I had always assumed that the old men's dreams here pointed to revelations distinctive of the older generation, and that the visions of young men pointed to different revelations distinctive of the younger generation. But I was suddenly struck by an altogether new possibility. Could this promise of God's outpoured Spirit be pointing to a unifying revelation whereby the dreams of old people and the visions of young people would merge, bringing them to a place of being in one accord as they together would behold the very same revelation of God?

This question, which was posed for me on that first night of the Spirit outpouring at Lee, has gripped me ever since. It has even tightened its grip as I have witnessed the continued outpourings of the Spirit on a host of other university campuses since the Asbury Outpouring. Could all these spiritual outpourings that have been sweeping across an entire generation, not unlike what transpired more than half a century ago in the Jesus Revolution,[28] be pointing and propelling us toward a spiritual outpouring that would sweep over and sweep together mothers and fathers and sons and daughters of all generations? Could this be a divine means to the end of an intergenerational turning of human hearts? Could this be some significant part of what all this means?

----

28. The term "Jesus Revolution" is the name of the feature film, starring Kelsey Grammer, which dramatizes the youth renewal movement of the 1970s. It premiered nationwide on February 24, 2023, which, quite remarkably, coincided with the last day of the sixteen-day span of the Asbury Outpouring.

The Holy Spirit and Spiritual Parenting

The key to spiritual parenting is the Holy Spirit. This final chapter makes explicit what has been implicit in all the previous chapters. Our success in spiritual parenting depends entirely upon the person and work of the Holy Spirit in our lives and our reliance upon the Spirit's presence and power.

This final chapter combines with the first chapter to form a theological frame around this study. In chapter 1 we considered the biblical roots of spiritual parenting and, here, in chapter 6, we will focus on the spiritual fruit. We saw how the roots are deeply grounded in God's role as the ultimate Father, revealed throughout Scripture and especially through His only begotten Son. We now turn to how Scripture makes clear that the fruit of spiritual parenting flourishes directly and entirely through the role of the Holy Spirit.

The Promise of the Father

We begin with a phrase Jesus used in reference to the Holy Spirit. He speaks of the gift of the Spirit as "the Promise of My Father." We first hear this phrase in the last chapter of Luke's Gospel where Jesus, in His last words to His disciples before His ascension, announces: "Behold, I send *the Promise of My Father* upon you; but tarry in the city of Jerusalem until you are endued with power from on high" (Luke 24:49, emphasis added). We hear this phrase again in the first chapter of Acts when Luke recalls Jesus's final instructions to His disciples: "And being assembled together with them, He commanded them not to depart from Jerusalem, but to wait for *the Promise of the Father*, 'which,' He said, 'you have heard from Me; for John truly baptized with water, but you shall be baptized with the Holy Spirit not many days from now'" (Acts 1:4–5, emphasis added).

Three verses later, Jesus expands upon these statements by making a major announcement about what will happen when this soon-coming "Promise of the Father" arrives: "You shall receive power when the Holy Spirit has come upon you; and you shall be witnesses to Me in Jerusalem, and in all Judea and Samaria, and to the end of the earth" (v. 8). This is a manifesto statement by Jesus that previews and projects the storyline of the rest of the book of Acts, and even the rest of the future history of the followers of Jesus up to our present day!

On the day of Pentecost, as recorded in Acts 2, Jesus's prediction reaches the moment of fulfillment. The Holy Spirit comes down and Peter stands up, as a freshly empowered witness himself, to announce this fulfillment: "This Jesus God has raised up, of which we are all witnesses. Therefore being exalted to the right hand of God, and having received from the Father the promise of the Holy Spirit, He poured out this which you now see and hear" (vv. 32–33).

As we all know, a witness sees something and speaks something. Something is beheld and something is told. Accordingly, the promise of the Holy Spirit has this juridical or judicial function to enable us to be witnesses—witnesses in the court of public opinion and before the throne of God, where Jesus is exalted. But why, then, should this impartation of the Holy Spirit be called "the promise *of the Father*" and not "the promise of the Lord" or "the promise of God" or "the promise of the Judge of all the earth"? I would suggest it is because God here is doing not only something *judicial* but also—and especially—something *parental*.

In fact, Peter leans into this when he comes down to the last recorded words of his Pentecost-day message, his altar call, if you will. "Repent," Peter says, "and let every one of you be baptized in the name of Jesus Christ for the remission of sins; and you shall receive the gift of the Holy Spirit. For the promise is to you *and to your children,* and to all who are afar off, as many as the Lord our God will call" (Acts 2:38–39, emphasis added). God is a parent, the ultimate and grandest parent, who is bestowing a gift that is meant to come down as a blessing upon His people. We can see this in terms of the parental blessing featured so prominently in the covenant of the Old Testament, as discussed previously in chapters 1 and 3.

This is the endowment, the inheritance that is meant to course down from parents to their children to their children's children and beyond. We see expanding impact here in Acts 2:39 (from "you" to "your children" to "all who are far off") much like we saw in Deuteronomy 6:6–19 (from "heart" to "home" to "city" to "nation"). This is the promise of the heavenly Father that is meant to be taken up by and passed down through every earthly mother and father. And it is the blessing that is ultimately destined to bless "all the families of the earth" (Gen. 12:3) and to reach unto "the uttermost part of the earth" (Acts 1:8 DRB).

A Promise for Parents

This whole notion of an inheritance of Spirit being passed through parent to child can remind us of Elisha's appeal to Elijah for "a double portion of your spirit" (2 Kings 2:9), as discussed in chapter 5. We remember that Israel's covenant called for a double share of the inheritance of property and land to go to the oldest son of the family. But in both 2 Kings 2 and Acts 2, an inheritance of Spirit, rather than physical property, is the issue. And in both cases, a wind comes down from heaven and transacts this endowment that goes beyond what is possible for any parent on earth. This is indeed *the promise of the Father from on high.*

In both Acts 2 and 2 Kings 2, there is something mysterious and wonderful in the way this wind, this Spirit from heaven, is seen both to differentiate and to bind together the different parties, particularly the different generations, upon whom it comes. In the story of 2 Kings 2, as we recall, a heavenly whirlwind comes down and separates Elijah from Elisha, yet it unites them spiritually in a parent-child bond: "My father, my father," Elisha exclaims from the vortex of this experience—an experience that leaves him clothed from on high with the mantle that descends from his elder (2 Kings 2:11–13).

In Acts 2, we see something similar. We see the wind rushing down with "divided tongues, as of fire" being distributed upon each one present (vv. 1–4), yet it draws all of them together into a bond of "one accord" (vv. 1, 46) that overrides human divisions—national, social, gender, and linguistic divisions, for sure (vv. 5–8, 16–18), but also the division between generations. We see this not only in Peter's previously noted statement (on the promise being "to you and to your children," v. 39) at the end of his message, but also in the defining declaration at the beginning of his message, when he says, "This is that which was spoken by the prophet Joel; And it shall come to pass in the last days, saith God, I will pour out my Spirit upon all flesh: and your sons and your daughters shall prophesy, your young men shall see visions, and your old men shall dream dreams'" (vv. 16–17 KJV; cf. Joel 2:28). Peter's Pentecost message, then, carries forward from Joel this powerful promise for parents—namely, that an overflowing endowment of the Holy Spirit is God's intended inheritance for them and for their children.

The Spirit's Intergenerational Work at the Beginning of Luke's Gospel

Peter announces the intergenerational promise of the Spirit at the beginning of the book of Acts, but the firstfruits of this promise can be seen in the intergenerational work of the Spirit at the beginning of Luke's Gospel, specifically in the birth stories we remember at Christmastime. In Luke's first two chapters, wherever we see the Holy Spirit mentioned we see a powerful connecting force moving on persons across generational lines. We see this first when Zechariah the priest receives the promise of a son, to be named John, who will be filled with the Holy Spirit from his mother's womb

(Luke 1:13–16). It is a spiritual endowment that is immediately linked to that of Elijah. In "the spirit and power of Elijah," the biblical text notes, this son named John will turn the hearts of elders to their children, echoing the canon-concluding prophecy of the book of Malachi (Luke 1:17; Mal. 4:6). The Spirit is coming not merely to empower individuals but to restore a connection that has been broken for an entire people, a lineage between elders and children through which the endowment of the Spirit can again wondrously flow.

From this point, Luke's Gospel promptly proceeds to narrate the ways in which the Holy Spirit begins to work in and around John to fulfill this promise of intergenerational reconnection. Even before John comes forth from his mother's womb, we see the Holy Spirit restoring this linkage between elders and children in multiple ways:

- In Zechariah receiving the promise of the Spirit for the destiny of his son John (Luke 1:13–17).
- In Elizabeth, in her old age, being filled with this son who is filled with the Spirit (vv. 15, 24–25).
- In Mary being told of her impregnation by the Holy Spirit in a revelation that immediately prompts her to go to her elder, Elizabeth (vv. 30–40).
- In these two women coming together, representing both young generation and old, each bearing through the Holy Spirit the seed of the next generation—coming together in a moment that totally explodes with the revelation of the Holy Spirit's intergenerational work of filling and overflowing the physical lineage of a people with a spiritual inheritance (vv. 39–56).

It is a prophetic moment when these two women from two different generations come together—one that, long before the day of Pentecost, begins to inaugurate the fulfillment of the intergenerational promise of Joel 2:28, which envisions the Spirit's prophetic gifts being poured out on sons and daughters, old and young, and menservants and maidservants:

- A son named John prophesies through a sign act of leaping in the womb of his mother, Elizabeth, who is herself then immediately filled with the Holy Spirit (Luke 1:41).
- A daughter named Mary prophesies a Magnificat of praise (vv. 46–55) for God's blessing upon her, "His maidservant," as she calls herself, directly echoing Joel's promise for "maidservants" (Joel 2:29; Acts 2:18). She predicts that her blessing will be acknowledged "henceforth [by] all generations" (Luke 1:48), and God's "mercy from generation to generation to all who fear him" (v. 50 NLT).
- Indeed, Mary is a maidservant who prophesies of how God "has helped his servant Israel," as He had promised "to our ancestors, to Abraham and his children forever" (vv. 54–55 NLT).

Thus, this moment of the *physical* convergence of three generations—Elizabeth, Mary, and their unborn children—becomes a moment that represents and reveals the *spiritual* convergence and connecting of generations including and extending far beyond these three, all the way back to Abraham and all the way forward to all his descendants throughout all of time to come.

And Luke's Gospel does not stop there, but goes on to describe subsequent moments that similarly represent and reveal this same kind of intergenerational work of the Spirit:

- We see this when John is brought for circumcision, and his father, Zechariah, in the solemn moment of recording his son's name, is filled with the Holy Spirit and begins to prophesy of his son's destiny (Luke 1:57–79).
- We see this when Mary and Joseph bring the infant Jesus into the temple before the old man Simeon, who had been led there "by the Spirit" at that very moment, as the biblical text notes, whereupon he prophesies of the destiny of the holy child (2:21–35).
- We see in these Spirit-infused moments of child dedication the fulfillment not only of old men's dreams, but also the dream of an old woman, Anna, the prophetess, who "coming in that instant" (v. 38a) when Simeon was prophesying over the infant Jesus, the biblical text says, "she gave thanks to God and spoke about the child to all who were looking forward to the redemption of Jerusalem" (v. 38b NIV).

If we step back and sum up this movement of the Spirit at the beginning of Luke's Gospel, we indeed see, from the birth announcement of John forward, the hearts of elders being turned to children. We see the Holy Spirit powerfully moving and filling elders around the events of these children's births and dedications, giving them visions and prophecies that illuminate the Spirit-endowed destinies of these children and the spiritual inheritance that all this bears and promises for all generations to come. All of this surely and rightfully can be described as the firstfruits of the promise—indeed, the promise *of the Father*. Thus, I would say this movement of the Spirit in the first two chapters of Luke cannot help but illuminate in this regard the movement of the Spirit in the first two chapters of Acts, where we see a much larger group of elders being filled with the Spirit and being given inspired promises concerning their sons and daughters and the spiritual inheritance that this outpouring of the Spirit is beginning to enact.

It is often observed that the book of Acts presents the outpouring of the Spirit issuing forth geographically through ever-widening regions of space (as Jesus Himself predicts: "in Jerusalem, and in all Judea, and in Samaria, and unto the uttermost part of the earth" [Acts 1:8 KJV]). Yet I think we have not given sufficient attention to the concern in Acts to see the outpouring of the Spirit issuing forth temporally through future generations—indeed, from generation to generation throughout all of time to come.

The Holy Spirit's Intergenerational Work Beyond the Family of Abraham

We need to notice one more important expectation that Luke's Gospel highlights. The Holy Spirit's intergenerational work is destined to move far beyond the family of Abraham. To be sure, this movement of the Spirit that we have been tracing, this promise of the Father, comes first to and through the lineage of "Abraham and his descendants forever" (NASB), as Mary prophesies (Luke 1:54–55) and "to His people," as Zechariah prophesies (v. 77; cf. vv. 16–17). Yet it is not destined to remain restricted to the physical lineage of Abraham. For as Simeon envisions in Luke 2, this salvation that has appeared to his eyes is being brought by God "before the face of all peoples, A light to bring revelation to the Gentiles," as well as "the glory of [God's] people, Israel" (vv. 30–32).

The promise of the Father is an outpouring of blessing so large, so enormous, so overflowing that it is destined from the beginning to spill over from Abraham's family to "all the families of the earth" (see Gen. 12:3 ESV). It is such a torrential promise that, as Peter, echoing Joel, declares, it is being poured out *"upon all flesh"* (Acts 2:17 KJV, emphasis added) and its range extends to *"whoever calls on the name of the LORD"* (v. 21, emphasis added). And so Peter, accordingly and finally, says to his audience of Jews *"from every nation under heaven,"* as they are described (v. 5 NIV, emphasis added): "The promise is for you and your children" but also, he adds, "and for all who are far off—for all whom the Lord our God will call" (v. 39 NIV).

Responding to the Call of the Spirit
Like Mary, the Mother of Jesus

The promise of the Father, then, is the gift of the Holy Spirit for parents and their children, even "for all who are far off—for all whom the Lord our God will call" (Acts 2:39 NIV). It is for certain that this reference to "all who are far off" is far-reaching enough to include anyone who is now reading the words of this book. In fact, I myself have thought of this book project, from start to finish, in terms of a call from the Spirit. As I explained in my introductory chapter, it all began for me as a call from the Spirit to *"Behold!"* And now in the light of all these chapters, I come to the end wanting to send it forth as a call to others to *"Behold and receive!"* Yes, receive the gift of the Holy Spirit that turns our hearts, reconnects the generations, and restores the fruitfulness of spiritual parenting!

When it comes to responding to this call of the Spirit, given what is presented so pointedly and powerfully in the message of Luke-Acts, I am led at last to the example of Mary, the mother of Jesus. After all, who on earth could ever be a greater example for us of spiritual parenting? Throughout this book we have acknowledged Scripture's emphasis upon *the fatherhood of God.* Yet our study of Scripture's witness on spiritual parenting will be sorely lacking if we fail to notice the place of primacy given to *the motherhood of Mary.*

The supreme place that Mary comes to occupy does not come from the volume of attention she is given in the biblical narrative. Her significance comes instead from the sheer enormity, singularity, and purity of her response to the call of the Spirit. We can see this in the biblical passage quoted at the beginning of this chapter. Here, Mary has just been told by the angel Gabriel, *"Behold,* you will conceive in your womb and bear a son, and you shall name him Jesus. He will be great and will be called the

Son of the Most High, and the Lord God will give him the throne of David his father" (Luke 1:31–32 NABRE, emphasis added). Obviously, Mary is here given the greatest spiritual parenting assignment in all of human history. Not only the enormity but also the impossibility of it all is not lost on her, and so she questions, "How will this be, since I am a virgin?" (v. 34 ESV). The answer: "The Holy Spirit will come upon you, and the power of the Most High will overshadow you; therefore the child to be born will be called holy—the Son of God" (v. 35 ESV). The Holy Spirit is the answer! The Holy Spirit is the answer that overshadows not only Mary's pregnancy but also the entire compass of her life and calling as the mother, the spiritual parent, of Jesus. And to this entire call of the Spirit, Mary responds: "*Behold*, I am the servant of the Lord; let it be to me according to your word" (v. 38 ESV, emphasis added).

The Holy Spirit was the answer for Mary in the face of her impossible spiritual parenting assignment. And the Holy Spirit is the answer for you, too, my dear reader! We might be tempted to place Mary on a pedestal so high that her parenting experience would be too lofty and too transcendent to be relevant and applicable to the rest of us mere mortals. But Gabriel's words to Mary include a statement that links her parenting experience to Elizabeth's and thereby brings the call of the Spirit back down to earth for her and for Elizabeth and, by extension, for all of us too, when he says, "And *behold*, your relative Elizabeth in her old age has also conceived a son, and this is the sixth month with her who was called barren. For nothing will be impossible with God" (vv. 36–37 ESV, emphasis added).

Notice the expansive range and future tense of this last statement by the angel Gabriel: "nothing will be impossible with God." This far-reaching claim encompasses both Mary's "thing" and Elizabeth's "thing," both then and on into the future—the future that even reaches all the way to us and any "thing" that might seem impossible in our call to be spiritual parents. This means that for this statement, too, it can be said, "[This] promise is for you and for your children and for all who are far off—for as many as the Lord our God shall call" (Acts 2:39 NIV). And so we can say, in response to our call to be spiritual parents, nothing less than what Mary said: "*Behold*, I am the servant of the Lord; let it be to me according to your word" (Luke 1:38 ESV, emphasis added).

A Devotional by My Daughter

My daughter Emily presented the following "Christmas Devotional" in December 2022 to a women's group in her local church congregation, the Ambassador Presbyterian Church in Apex, North Carolina. Although unforeseen when she composed and first delivered it, the message of this devotional now forms a fitting conclusion to the final chapter of this book. And the intergenerational spirit of its message provides an appropriate and illustrative ending to the book as a whole. As you will see, this devotional reflects not only the spirit of Christmas but also the Spirit of spiritual parenting.

"Christmas Devotional"
by Emily Moore Young

Advent season is one of my favorite times of year because it is a season of stories—the Bible stories of Christ's coming to earth, of course, but also our stories. We send Christmas cards with our years in review. Those of us with kids—like so many in our larger culture—spend lots of time telling stories about Santa, the naughty list, reindeer, and elves on shelves. We gather in groups with our families and friends to watch Christmas movies, reminisce about the past, share holiday memories, and retell the stories that convey our faith and give meaning to our shared experiences.

I tend to think quite a lot about stories. I teach English and work as an editor in my two part-time "joblets," as I call them. My primary role these days is being a mommy to my three kids, and that also involves lots of storytelling! Reading books together, telling Bible stories, hearing my kids talk about and make sense of the events of their days, reinforcing family rules with stories that give them context. One of my kids' favorite things is to hear stories about my childhood. And I believe this appetite for stories is a universal, human trait. We are born to love stories and created to learn from them.

When I was a little girl, I loved to hear my parents' stories. Each night at bedtime, my dad would snuggle up next to me in bed and offer me a choice: I could hear him tell me a story from his imagination (I can still remember many of these—ask me sometime about "The Duck That Went to Church"); a story from his childhood (usually involving the mischievous shenanigans of him and my uncle); or a story from the Bible. Now, that third option might seem boring by comparison, but my dad is legendary for his deep and vivid way of retelling stories from Scripture!

So, on one particular night when I was about five years old, I told my dad that I would like to hear a Bible story. He thought for a minute, then jumped up and ran out of the room. After a minute, he came back, snuggled beside me on the bed, and proceeded to begin the story of Saul on the Damascus Road, on his way to persecute some early followers of Jesus—the story that leads up to Saul's conversion to Paul. Now my dad ad-libbed the story for me, but here is how it begins in the book of Acts, chapter 9:

> Meanwhile, Saul was still breathing out murderous threats against the Lord's disciples. He went to the high priest and asked him for letters to the synagogues in Damascus, so that if he found any there who belonged to the Way, whether men or women, he might take them as prisoners to Jerusalem. As he neared Damascus on his journey, suddenly a light from heaven flashed around him. He fell

to the ground and heard a voice say to him, "Saul, Saul, why do you persecute me?"

"Who are you, Lord?" Saul asked.

"I am Jesus, whom you are persecuting," he replied. "Now get up and go into the city, and you will be told what you must do." (Acts 9:1–6 NIV)

Well, my dad didn't make it through the entire story, because when he got to the part about a bright light appearing in the sky, suddenly a bright light appeared on the ceiling of my bedroom! It was the most terrifying thing that had ever happened to me up to that point in my life! And rather than being captivated by my dad's story, I was suddenly thrown into a panic, because I thought God was about to burst through the roof and into my room!

So, I'm screaming from fright. My mom, who can hear the commotion reverberating through the house, is yelling at my dad, and my dad is trying to suppress his laughter, to comfort me, and to show me that the "light from heaven" was actually from a flashlight he had hidden by the bedside for some story-time special effects. He had wanted to bring the Bible to life, but instead he had unintentionally hurled me into the mortifying belief that I was about to die! I will never forget the relief I felt when I realized that the heavens weren't actually opening up into my bedroom.

Remembering this story of a storytelling experience brings to my mind the stories of Advent and Christmas recorded in the Gospel of Luke, when heaven really did come down to announce Christ's coming. When the angel appeared to the shepherds in Bethlehem, they, like I myself on that night, were overwhelmed with fear. So the first thing the angel had to say to them was "Fear not" (Luke 2:8–10 KJV). This is also one of the first things Gabriel said to Mary when he appeared to her in Luke, which incidentally, is the beginning of Mary's Advent season. Here is how Luke 1:26–55 (NIV) records this part of the Christmas story:

> In the sixth month of Elizabeth's pregnancy, God sent the angel Gabriel to Nazareth, a town in Galilee, to a virgin pledged to be married to a man named Joseph, a descendant of David. The virgin's name was Mary. The angel went to her and said, "Greetings, you who are highly favored! The Lord is with you."
>
> Mary was greatly troubled at his words and wondered what kind of greeting this might be. But the angel said to her, "Do not be afraid, Mary; you have found favor with God. You will conceive and give birth to a son, and you are to call him Jesus. He will be great and will be called the Son of the Most High. The Lord God will give him the throne of his father David, and he will reign over Jacob's descendants forever; his kingdom will never end."

"How will this be," Mary asked the angel, "since I am a virgin?"

The angel answered, "The Holy Spirit will come on you, and the power of the Most High will overshadow you. So the holy one to be born will be called the Son of God. Even Elizabeth your relative is going to have a child in her old age, and she who was said to be unable to conceive is in her sixth month. For no word from God will ever fail."

"I am the Lord's servant," Mary answered. "May your word to me be fulfilled." Then the angel left her.

At that time Mary got ready and hurried to a town in the hill country of Judea, where she entered Zechariah's home and greeted Elizabeth. When Elizabeth heard Mary's greeting, the baby leaped in her womb, and Elizabeth was filled with the Holy Spirit. In a loud voice she exclaimed: "Blessed are you among women, and blessed is the child you will bear! But why am I so favored, that the mother of my Lord should come to me? As soon as the sound of your greeting reached my ears, the baby in my womb leaped for joy. Blessed is she who has believed that the Lord would fulfill his promises to her!" And Mary said:

"My soul glorifies the Lord
　and my spirit rejoices in God my Savior,

for he has been mindful
    of the humble state of his servant.
From now on all generations will call me
    blessed,
    for the Mighty One has done great things
    for me—
    holy is his name.
His mercy extends to those who fear him,
    from generation to generation.
He has performed mighty deeds with his arm;
    he has scattered those who are proud in
    their inmost thoughts.
He has brought down rulers from their thrones
    but has lifted up the humble.
He has filled the hungry with good things
    but has sent the rich away empty.
He has helped his servant Israel,
    remembering to be merciful
to Abraham and his descendants forever,
    just as he promised our ancestors."

So, in this story, the angel Gabriel appeared, and Mary was "greatly troubled" in spirit (v. 29)—in other words, she was "very afraid," as indicated in Gabriel's immediate directive: "Do not be afraid" (v. 30). God sent his angelic messenger to invite a young woman to be a part of this most amazing and altogether *true* story in history. She would conceive a son who would be the long-awaited Messiah. She was given a promise, and although it had not yet come to pass, she believed. Belief replaced her fear. And what was her next step in response to her belief? After the angel departed, she hurried on her way to visit Elizabeth, probably intending to tell her the amazing news—yes, to tell Elizabeth her story!

Then, when she reached Elizabeth, her heart overflowed with amazement, and she was moved to give praise to the Lord. She suddenly had an awareness that she was being drawn up into a world-changing story—one with a backstory that long predated her (according to verse 55 [NIV]: "just as he promised our ancestors")—and she recognized that it was a historic, cosmic, and forward-reaching story that would be retold for all generations to come (according to verse 48 [NIV]: "From now on all generations will call me blessed").

Yet unlike Mary's response of belief and faithful expectation, Saul on his way to Damascus had not believed or received the Messiah. He believed Jesus of Nazareth to be the heretic, the rabble-rouser, the instigator of controversy. It's not until Saul was suddenly halted on his way to Damascus, when the heavens opened and a great light appeared, that his Advent moment finally arrived.

Saul was blinded by this heavenly light that suddenly appeared there on the road. And then Saul heard God's voice speaking to him and giving him instructions that propelled the story forward, as recorded in Acts 9:6-22 (NIV):

"Now get up and go into the city, and you will be told what you must do."

The men traveling with Saul stood there speechless; they heard the sound but did not see anyone. Saul got up from the ground, but when he opened his eyes he could see nothing. So they led him by the hand into Damascus. For three days he was blind and did not eat or drink anything.

In Damascus there was a disciple named Ananias. The Lord called to him in a vision, "Ananias!"

"Yes, Lord," he answered.

The Lord told him, "Go to the house of Judas on Straight Street and ask for a man from Tarsus named Saul, for he is praying. In a vision he has seen a man named Ananias come and place his hands on him to restore his sight."

"Lord," Ananias answered, "I have heard many reports about this man and all the harm he has done to your holy people in Jerusalem. And he has come here with authority from the chief priests to arrest all who call on your name."

But the Lord said to Ananias, "Go! This man is my chosen instrument to proclaim my name to the Gentiles and their kings and to the people of Israel. I will show him how much he must suffer for my name."

Then Ananias went to the house and entered it. Placing his hands on Saul, he said, "Brother Saul, the Lord—Jesus, who appeared to you on the road as you were coming here—has sent me so that you may see again and be filled with the Holy Spirit." Immediately, something like scales fell from Saul's eyes, and he could see again. He got up and was baptized, and after taking some food, he regained his strength.

Saul spent several days with the disciples in Damascus. At once he began to preach in the synagogues that Jesus is the Son of God. All those who heard him were astonished and asked, "Isn't he the man who raised havoc in Jerusalem among those who call on this name? And hasn't he come here to take them as prisoners to the chief priests?" Yet Saul grew more and more powerful and baffled the Jews living in Damascus by proving that Jesus is the Messiah.

Jesus Christ came down from heaven in a blinding bright light to encounter Saul, who was told to go and wait in blindness for three days. Then Ananias arrived, and Paul was made new! New name! New sight! New heart! Filled with the Holy Spirit! And empowered to go forth and preach the gospel! That's what the coming of Jesus did for Paul, and what His coming offers each of us—a transformed identity, a transformed heart, and a transformed life.

I have always felt an affinity with this Bible story, ever since that night in my childhood bed. I have been able to understand the fear and awe that Paul must have felt, because in my own five-year-old way, I had experienced it too. At the time, I was relieved that God had not actually burst through my ceiling and into my room.

However, from my current vantage point, I can now see that Jesus *did* actually come into my room that night and into my heart. His presence gripped me with the arresting conviction that at any moment God could, and truly might, show up in my room—yes, in my life, to speak to me. And, in light of this, my life has never been the same.

God used that bedtime story, along with the countless other biblical and personal stories that my parents told me, to cultivate in my heart an openness to God's holy and awesome and loving presence. And I pray that this season will be, for all of us, a time of hopeful expectation of Christ's presence here with us, opening our eyes, speaking to our hearts, and transforming our fears into faith. So that in this season we can join in Mary's Advent song, worshipping God and saying, "Our souls glorify the Lord, and our spirits rejoice in God our Savior, for He has been mindful of the humble state of His servants. The Mighty One has done great things for us—holy is His name!" (see Luke 1:46–49).

SELECT BIBLIOGRAPHY WITH ANNOTATIONS

Anthony, Michelle. *Spiritual Parenting: An Awakening for Today's Families* (David C. Cook, 2010).

This volume, written by the pastor of children and parents of New Life Church in Colorado Springs, Colorado, combines biblical insight, seasoned parenting experience, and practical guidance in faith formation. Emphasis is placed upon an approach to parenting that leans heavily on God's promised guidance and help, rather than a fear-oriented focus on managing and controlling the behavior of one's children. The book's main chapters identify various environments of faith into which we can lead our children as we seek and trust in the Spirit's work to turn their hearts to a transforming faith and a vital relationship with God.

Hanby, Mark with Craig Lindsay Ervin. *You Have Not Many Fathers: Recovering the Generational Blessing* (Destiny Image Publishers, 1996).

This book, authored by a spiritual father with the assistance of one of his spiritual sons, takes its title from Paul's words in 1 Corinthians 4:15—"For though you might have ten thousand instructors in Christ, yet you do not have many fathers." As Hanby explains in the book's opening "Acknowledgment," most of the book's content was compiled by Ervin from recorded messages that Hanby delivered over the course of many years in Christian ministry as a pastor, an evangelist, and an internationally recognized conference speaker. As Hanby further explains in his "Introduction," the book's content emerged from his own path of personal repentance, involving extensive searching of Scripture and soul-searching response to God's call in his own life to turn away from inadequate models of ministry leadership and toward what he shows to be the biblical pattern of spiritual parenting, as revealed in the ministry of Paul, the life of Elijah, and the ultimate divine revelation of the Father and Son. Although Hanby is especially concerned with the mentoring of persons with ministerial callings, the biblical patterns he freshly explicates have relevance for the complete range of intergenerational relationships.

Kreider, Larry. *The Cry for Spiritual Mothers & Fathers: The Next Generation Needs You to Be a Spiritual Mentor* (Regal, 2014).

Kreider, the founder and director of DOVE Christian Fellowship International, has here written one of the most practical and instructive books available on spiritual parenting. This book carries forward and expands upon his two previous books on the topic, published in

2000 and 2008. Thoroughly informed by Scripture and by Kreider's extensive firsthand practice and promotion of spiritual parenting, the chapters of this book are presented in three major parts, which respectively address: (1) the importance of spiritual parenting for everyone; (2) the path of becoming a spiritual mother or father; and (3) practical insights for developing and meeting the challenges of spiritual parenting. Kreider makes a strong case for the claim that "everyone is called to be a spiritual mother or father," and he also promotes, in what he has both taught and practiced, that spiritual parenting is a defining dimension of the life of the church.

McClung, Floyd. *The Father Heart of God* (David C. Cook, 2022).

This Christian classic was first published in 1985, and now there are more than one million copies in print in thirty-two different languages. McClung, who worked for many years as a global missionary leader and pioneered multiple mission organizations on four continents, began his work in Youth With A Mission, eventually becoming YWAM's international executive director. Drawing upon his extensive ministry with youth, McClung addresses the father wounds that plague the younger generation. With discerning biblical insight and pastoral sensitivity, he lays out the specific steps to healing through personal encounter with the father heart of God. This current reprint features a foreword by Pete Greig, who references his own personal story of how McClung's book impacted his life in his teens and how McClung himself became "a father in God" to him in his early thirties.

This book is particularly instructive on the crucial role that forgiveness plays in this heart-transforming work of the heavenly Father.

Murray, Andrew. *Raising Your Children for Christ* (Whitaker House, 2017).

Murray, a South African pastor in the Dutch Reform Church in the late nineteenth and early twentieth centuries, became well-known for his prolific writing of Christian devotional literature. He published more than fifty books, many of which became widely republished classics of Christian devotion, including this book on spiritual parenting. It was originally published under the title *The Children for Christ* in 1887. This book presents fifty brief chapters, each beginning with a featured Scripture passage sequenced in canonical order (half from the Old Testament and half from the New Testament), followed by commentary on each given passage and a concluding prayer. This volume is rich in biblical insight, devotional nourishment, and timeless wisdom on spiritual parenting.

Smalley, Gary and John Trent. *The Blessing* (Pocket Books, Simon & Schuster, 1986).

This book, written by two Christian counselors, presents a widely noted study of the parental practice of bestowing blessing upon one's children. Relevant to spiritual parenting in both the family and the church, this study combines insights drawn from Scripture, from Jewish tradition, and from extensive contemporary family counseling experience. The authors emphasize the crucial need in our time for recovering this biblical practice. Separate chapters are devoted to various practical aspects of parental blessing. These include: "meaningful touch, a spoken message, attaching 'high value' to the one being blessed, picturing a special future to the one being blessed, and an active commitment to fulfill the blessing."

Thomas, Gary. *Sacred Parenting: How Raising Children Shapes Our Souls*. Revised ed. (Zondervan, 2017).

Thomas has long been a leading voice in American evangelical circles in the areas of marriage and family relationships. He has gained wide notoriety as a teacher, speaker, and author of numerous books, including a signature work entitled *Sacred Marriage: What If God Designed Marriage to Make Us Holy More Than to Make Us Happy?* (Zondervan, 2000). Turning his attention now to *Sacred Parenting,* Thomas approaches this endeavor from the same spiritual angle and offers a treatment that is fresh and rich in biblical and theological insight. Thomas points out that he, like Scripture itself on the topic, is not primarily concerned with the "how-to" but rather with the "what for" and the "why" of parenting.